Con REDEMPTION

The Hidden Truth

Copyright © 2009
by
David E. Robinson

All Rights Reserved
Parts of this book may be reproduced subject to due
and specific acknowledgment of their source.

Maine-Patriot.com
3 Linnell Circle
Brunswick, Maine 04011

maine-patriot.com

"Forgive us our debts, as we forgive our debtors." — *Matthew 6:12.*

Commercial REDEMPTION
The Hidden Truth

Contents

1. The Wizard Of OZ --- 7
2. Two Laws --- 19
3. Two States --- 23
4. Two Men --- 29
5. Divine Right Of Kings --- 35
6. Constitutional Freedoms --- 39
7. Two Men, Revisited --- 43
8. Two Laws, Revisited --- 45
9. Four Laws --- 47
10. Three United States --- 51
11. Unlimited Power To Contract --- 55
12. Mark Of The Beast --- 57
13. The Conversion --- 61
14. The Strawman --- 67
15. Manmade v. Real --- 75
16. Administrative Law --- 83
17. Public Bankruptcy --- 89
18. The Commercial Game --- 93
19. The Private Domain --- 107
20. Your Name Is Your Bond --- 113

21	Know Who You Are	123
22	Redemption In Law	127
23	Who Am I?	131
24	Working With Drafts	139
25	A Knight's Tale	149
26	The London Joust	159
27	The Real Game In Town	169
28	Public v. Private	173
29	New World Order? Or Release	177
30	Redemption & The Lord's Release	181
31	The Passover	191
32	Redemption & Jubilee	199
33	Maxims Of Law	201

1
The Wizard of OZ

An Allegory is the expression of truths about human conduct and experience by means of symbolic fictional figures and actions.

Such was the movie *The Wizard of Oz,* an allegory of the state of affairs we now live in today — an allegory of the unfolding New World Order that was instituted in America via the stock-market crash of 1929 and the bankruptcy of the United States in 1933.

The setting of this allegory is in Kansas — the "heartland" of America; the geographical center of the U.S.A.

In came the twister — the whirling confusion of the Great Depression, the stock-market crash, the U.S. Bankruptcy, and the theft of America's gold — that whisked Dorothy and Toto up into the New Order of the World; an artificial new dimension *"somewhere, over the rainbow,"* above the solid ground of Kansas.

When they landed in Oz, Dorothy commented to her little dog Toto: *"Toto? I have a feeling we're not in Kansas anymore . . ."*

Exactly!

After the bankruptcy of the United States, Kansas was no longer "Kansas" anymore, it is now "KS" — a two-capital-letter federal postal designation that is part of the "federal zone," designated by the **Z**one **I**m**P**rovement (ZIP) Code established by the bankrupt United States in 1933 — and Dorothy and Toto were now "in this state." The terms: "in this state," "this state," and "state" are deceptively defined for tax jurisdiction purposes as the "District of Columbia," a.k.a. the United

The Hidden Truth 7

States, Inc., or the corporate United States.

In the 1930s the all-capital-letter-written-name strawman — the newly created artificial "person" that has no brain and speaks and acts for its once-upon-a-time sovereign, you and me — was created while Americans were confused and distracted by the commotion caused by the introduction of the New World Order of communistic socialism, to figure out that they even had a strawman with which to contend. The scarecrow identified this <u>strawman persona</u> for Dorothy thusly: "*Some people without brains do an awful lot of talking. Of course, I'm not bright about* doing *things.*"

In his classic song, *"If I Only Had A Brain,"* the scarecrow/strawman succinctly augured, *"I'd unravel every riddle, For every Individdle, In trouble or in pain."*

Individual: a United States government Employee. (*Title 5 USC §552(a)2*). The Internal Revenue Code (IRC) and all state tax codes are in harmony with the above definition of "individual" by reference only. A <u>Corporation-of-one</u> is an artificial person constructed by law; not a living, breathing man or woman. An "individual" is a public corporate persona existing only in the public (*government*) domain having been created by law, not by God.

The drafters of codes and laws take everyday common speech and give it arcane encrypted meanings that are generally unknown or unknowable to the uninitiate even after serious study. Therefore, most folks are commercially, legally, and financially enslaved because of their ignorance of the true situation. Even knowing that "ignorance of the law is no excuse" they find themselves helpless, unarmed, and uninformed.

Translation: Once we discover that our strawman exists, and that we have co-signed for him, political and legal mysteries, complexities, and confusions are resolved. When we take title to our strawman, we protect ourselves from any liabilities that we might otherwise occur.

The tin-man, our **T**axpayer-**I**dentification-**N**umber (TIN) man, is a hollow man of tin, a vessel, or vehicle; newly created code word*s* for our strawman.

Just as the strawman has no brain, the tin-man vessel/vehicle has no heart. Both are artificial persons. (*person = persona = mask*).

Persons are divided by law into natural and artificial. Natural persons are persons created by God, and artificial persons are persons devised by human law for the purpose of governing them as "corporations-of-one" or bodies-politic.

The precise definition of the term "person" is therefore necessary to identify those to whom the 14th Amendment to the Constitution affords its protections and liabilities, since the 14th Amendment expressly applies to "persons."

A strawman is a person with a fictitious name written in "legalese" — language foreign to the rules of English grammar. Men and women with names written in cursive, with initial-letters-only capitalized, are not "persons" even though they are referred to as natural persons at times.

It is as impossible for a person to be natural as it is for a man to be artificial. "Person" is a silent artificial construct hatched up by lawyers, to be used and controlled by lawyers encrypted "codes."

One of the definitions of **"tin"** in Webster's dictionary is "counterfeit." The tin-man represents the mechanical and heartless aspect of commerce and commercial law. Just like they say in the Mafia, as they throw you overboard, *"Nothing personal; it's just business."*

The heartless tin-man carried an "axe," a traditional symbol for God, and for modern commercial law, in most dominant civilizations, including fascist states. In the words of the tin-man, as he expressed relief after Dorothy had oiled his arm, *"I've held that axe up for ages."*

The word "ace" is etymologically related to the word "axe" and in a deck of cards the *only* card above the King is the Ace; God. One of the Axis Powers of World War II was a fascist state, Italy. The symbol for fascism is the "fasces," a bundle of rods with an ax bound up in it with its blade sticking out.

The fasces may be found on the reverse of the American Mercury-head dime (*the Roman deity Mercury was the God of Commerce*) and on the wall behind and on each side of the Speaker's Podium in the United States House, each gold *fasces* being approximately six feet high. At the base of the Seal of the United States Senate are two fasces, crossed.

The lion in the story represents the "at-one-time" fearless American people as having lost their courage. And after a round with the IRS, in "defending" your *T-I-N man, dummy corporation, vessel vehicle, individual employee, public corporation, all capital letters written name, artificial person,* strawman, you'd lose your courage, too. You perhaps haven't *known* it, but the IRS has been dealing with you all along via your tin-man under the hidden laws of commerce. Just like the tin-man, "commerce" has no heart; it is heartless.

To find the Wizard, you have to *"follow the yellow-brick road"* (*the gold-bar road*). Follow the trail of America's stolen gold and you'll find the thief who stole it.

In the beginning of the movie, the Wizard's counterpart was the traveling mystic, "Professor Marvel," who Dorothy encountered when she ran away with Toto. His macabre shingle touted that he was "acclaimed by The Crowned Heads of Europe, Past, Present, and Future." Professor Marvel must have *really* been a Wizard to be acclaimed so by the future Crowned Heads of Europe, even before they were crowned!

Before the bankers stole America, they had long-since overpowered the Christian Kings and Queens of Europe and looted their kingdoms. Maybe "Professor Marvel" knew something about the future that other folks didn't know. With a human skull peering down from its painted perch above the door to his wagon, the professor lectured Dorothy about the priests of Isis and Osiris, the Paraohs of Egypt, and the days of yore.

When Dorothy Gale and her new friends emerged from the forest, they were elated to see the Emerald City before them, only a short distance away. The Wicked Witch of the West, desperate for the ruby slippers that Dorothy was wearing, would have to make her move before our heroes arrived safely inside the Emerald City gates.

In the original book, *The Wonderful Wizard of Oz,* by Frank Baum, published 39 years before the movie came out in 1939, and three years before the crash, the slippers were not *ruby-red,* but *silver.*

America still had its gold at that time, and the value of 1 oz. of gold was set at 15 ozs. of silver; silver being the more plentiful. Backed by gold, the currency carried America to a position of pre-eminence throughout the world. But when the movie came out in 1939, the slippers were not silver, but ruby red.

Between 1916 and 1933, America's gold was absorbed by the private non-federal Federal Reserve and shipped off to the FED owners in Germany and England because the use of Federal Reserve Notes carried an interest penalty that could only be paid in gold. Our *former* currency, United States Notes, carried no such interest requirement, but such was the "bargain" that came with the New World Order of the non-federal Federal Reserve in 1913.

When the United States' Bankruptcy was declared in 1933, Americans were forced to turn in (*surrender*) all their gold coin, gold bullion, and gold certificates by May 1st — *"May Day"* — the birthday of the Communism and the Illuminati in 1776, the year that the American Colonists declared their independence from the Crown.

Talking to people who were alive at that time, the general sentiment toward such "theft" in 1933 bordered on a second revolutionary war.

Maybe it was too much of a clue, or too much salt in their wounds, for Dorothy to be skipping down the golden yellow-brick-road in a pair of silver slippers. So, for whatever reason, a color less likely to provoke the people was selected.

With regard to the choice of ruby slippers — slippers colored red — one explanation is that on commercial documents and the like, red signifies private as opposed to public. Your new Social Security Card has a red serial number on the reverse. But no matter their color in the movie, the Wicked Witch of the West had big plans to get her hands on the precious slippers before Dorothy and crew could make it to Emerald City.

Her tactic was to drug them into unconsciousness by covering the countryside with poppy flowers, poppies — the source of heroin, opium, and morphine —

and then waltz in and snatch the slippers. In other words, the best way to loot the gold was to dull the senses of the American people with a contrived crisis (*the Great Depression*).

The poppy-drugs worked on Dorothy, the lion and Toto — the flesh-and-blood entities — but had no effect on the scarecrow or the tin-man — the artificial entities. The two cried out for help, and Glenda — the Good Witch of the North — answered their cries with a blanket of snow that nullified the narcotic effect of the poppies on Dorothy, Toto, and the lion.

As they all scampered toward the Emerald City — the city of green non-federal Federal Reserve Notes (*the new fiat money, money by decree*) — we hear the Munchkins singing the glories of the Wizard's Creation:

"*You're out of the woods, Your out of the dark, Your out of the night. Step into the sun, Step into the light, Keep straight ahead for the most glorious place on the face of the earth or the stars!*"

This jingle abounds with Illuminati/Luciferian metaphors regarding darkness and light.

The Wicked Witch of the West made her home in a round medieval Watchtower — ancient symbol of The Knights Templar of Freemasonry who are given to practicing witchcraft and are also credited to be the originators of modern banking, circa 1099 A.D.

The Wicked Witch of the West was dressed in black, the color that symbolizes the planet Saturn, a sacred icon of The Knights Templar, and the "color of choice" of judges and priests for their robes.

Who was the Wicked Witch of the West? Remember, in the first part of the film her counterpart was Almira Gulch who, according to Aunt Em, "owned half the county." Miss. Gulch alleged that Dorothy's dog, Toto, had bitten her. She came to the farm with an "order from the Sheriff" demanding that they surrender Toto to her custody and control. Aunt Em was not immediately cooperative and answered Miss. Gulch's allegations that Toto had bitten her, "*He's really gentle; with gentle (gentile) people, that is.*"

When Miss. Gulch challenged them to withhold Toto from her and *"go against the law,"* dear old Aunt Em was relegated to "pushing the Party Line" for Big Brother government. Aunt Em dutifully succumbed to the pressure and counselled Dorothy, reluctantly, "We can't go against the law, Dorothy. I'm afraid poor Toto will have to go."

When Dorothy refused to surrender Toto, Miss Gulch lashed out: *"If you don't hand over that dog I'll bring a suit that'll take your whole farm!"*

Today 70% of all attorneys in the world reside in the West — in America to be exact — and 95% of all law suites in the world are filed under the Jurisdiction of the corporate United States. The Wicked Witch of the West and Miss. Gulch symbolize Judges and Attorneys — primary agents for the transfer of all wealth in America from the people to the United States, the United Nations, and the international banks.

The American Bar Association is a branch of the Bar Council, under the Bar Association of England and Wales. As the copyrighted property of a British Company, all states' and United States Codes are private British owned Law, and all states' and United States courts, state Bar Associations, and the "State of [each of the 50 States]," go by and enforce private *de facto* British owned Law against Americans, operating as private foreign owned tribunals or administrative agencies doing business in the states under cover and color of [each of the 50 states'] Law.

The Wicked Witch of the West wanted the ruby (*silver*) slippers (*the precious metals*) — and her counterpart, Miss. Gulch, wanted Toto, too. What does "toto" signify in attorney legalese? "Everything!" Miss. Gulch wanted to take everything.

Dorothy and the gang fell for the Wizard's illusion in the beginning, but soon wised up and discovered the Wizard for what he was, a confidence man. When asked about helping the scarecrow/strawman, the Wizard cited — among other *babblings* about "getting a brain" and "universities" — the land of "E Pluribus Unum" (*Latin for "One out of many"*); converting many into one; meaning the New World Order.

"Novus Ordo Seclorum" is the Latin phrase placed on the American one-dollar bill shortly after the bankruptcy of the U.S. Government was declared in 1933. The Wizard proudly revealed (*confessed*) that he was: *"Born and bred in the heart of the western wilderness; an old Kansas man myself."*

The bankers did quite well. And, as the Wizard said, they made a killing in the America' west with the theft of America's gold, labor, and property from the *"grateful and responsive rural folk"* (*a quoted phrase of John D. Rockefeller*) who populated the country at that time.

When Dorothy asked Glenda, the Good Witch of the North for help in getting back to Kansas, Glenda replied, *"You don't need to be helped; you've always had the power to go back to Kansas."*

Translation: You've always had the right and power to re-claim your sovereignty, you just forgot your remedy; a UCC Form and Security Agreement sent to the Secretary of State and an Invoice and Bill of Exchange to the Secretary of the Treasury, that can be completed from scratch in a very short time.

Remedy: Remedy is the means by which the violation of a right is prevented, redressed, or compensated.

Both remedy and rights include those remedial rights of self-help which are among the most important bodies of rights under the Universal Commercial Code (UCC). Remedial rights are rights an aggrieved party can resort to on his own. "Acceptance of Value" is our Remedy.

Americans have intimate firsthand knowledge of the heartless mechanics of the laws of commerce when strictly applied by the unregistered, foreign agents of the IRS.

The Internal Revenue Service is the collection agency for the private non-federal Federal Reserve and the International Monetary Fund. It was placed under the Uniform Commercial Code in 1954 and has been operating strictly in that realm ever since.

You may have wondered about the meaning behind the words *The Wizard of Oz*. Look them up in the dictionary. Like almost everything else, the ruse is out there in the open for all to see, if you will look, and see.

One definition of Wizard is "a person of high professional skill or knowledge." Oz is an abbreviation of "onza," the Italian word for ounce (oz.) or ounces, the unit of measurement of gold and silver and other precious metals. No matter how large the quantity of gold or silver being discussed, the amount is always expressed in ounces rather than hundreds of tons of gold, its stated as so many million ounces of gold.

As the factual history of this country attests, *The Wizard of Oz* is the *Wizard of Ounces,* of silver and gold.

Everything worked out for Dorothy (*the American*

people) in the end. In the end she "made it home" to Kansas and her friends.

Meaning: There's a **remedy** encoded, disguised, and camouflaged in law. The UCC has been cracked and there's a way home, just like in the movie. Like Dorothy said, "There's no place like home" — there's nothing like sovereignty for a sovereign!

Vice Admiralty courts are courts established in the Queen's possessions beyond the seas, with jurisdiction over maritime causes and those relating to "prize." The United States is now a colony (*a possession*) of the English Crown, per a joint commercial venture agreement between the colonies (*the United States*) and the Crown, that brought the United States back under British ownership and rule, in 1933.

But the American people had a "standing in law" as sovereigns, independent of any connection to the United States and the Crown. This "standing in law" necessitated that the people be brought back under British rule, quietly and one at a time — but the Commercial Process of Redemption, through the UCC, will redeem us from this travesty.

All courts in America are Vice-Admiralty courts conducting the private *foreign* commerce of the Crown. But there is commercial remedy in Redemption-in-Law.

Will you continue to be conned by confidence men into worshiping the Wizard's light-show (*the Apocalypse Beast*) — or will you look behind the veil?

2
Two Laws

*"Render to Caesar the <u>things that **are** Caesar's</u>, and to God the <u>things that **are** God's</u>."* — Mark 12:17.

"Render to Caesar" is often quoted as the definitive answer to how much authority Caesar has over us. But does something belong to Caesar simply because he says it does? For example, if the income tax rate is raised to 100%, do we hand over our entire paycheck to Caesar? If not, what number is the magical dividing line above which Caesar is asking too much and we are allowed to hold back the remainder for God and our own needs? A meaningful answer, if there is one, cannot come in the form of something as arbitrary as a percentage point.

There is a clear answer, and it can be found hiding within the very structure of modern law.

Two Laws

Since law is an area that few will ever study, some background is necessary. We will use the country of New Zealand as a for instance, and reveal an **illusion** at work that keeps most people ignorant of how the law really works.

For starters, "the law" is presented as a singular beast that you are either obeying or not obeying — when in fact, all English speaking nations have at least two distinct systems of law operating at one and the same time.

Statutory "Law" (or Statutes)

The law we are all familiar with consists of millions of pages of statutory regulations governing every aspect imaginable of modern life, from taxes to car registration, to protecting the environment. We either deal with these laws as an accepted part of life, or hear about their effect on us regularly. Elected officials get to sit in the Capitol and decide what is best for us, and alter the laws according to their whims.

In New Zealand, the latest evil politicians are determined to eradicate through "law" is bovine flatulence.

So if Caesar says the air is his and cows are no longer allowed to pollute it, a new statute removes the air from God's domain and places it under Caesar's jurisdiction. If you don't like it, all you can do is vote for someone who might do better — or worse.

For some reason that no one can explain, the trend is for these laws to get less beneficial, and more costly over time.

Compare the ever changing nature of these laws with a well known example from scripture:

*"Then they came near, and spake before the king concerning the king's decree; Hast thou not signed a decree, that every man that shall ask **a petition** of any God or man within thirty days, save of thee, O king, shall be cast into the den of lions? The king answered and said, The thing is true, according to **the law** of the Medes and Persians, which **altereth not**. Then answered they and said before the king, That Daniel, which is of the children of the captivity of Judah, regardeth not thee, O king, nor the decree that thou hast signed, but maketh his petition three*

*times a day. Then the king, when he heard these words, was sore displeased with himself, and set his heart on Daniel to deliver him: and he laboured till the going down of the sun to deliver him. Then these men assembled unto the king, and said unto the king, Know, O king, that the law of the Medes and Persians is, That **no decree ... which the king establisheth may be changed**."* (Daniel 6:12-15).

How is it that king Darius, the ruler of a vast empire, could not change his own law when he clearly wanted to, yet our legislatures simply have to cast a majority vote and the rules change again? Which one of these is consistent with the definition of the word "law?"

LAW: "n. [L. lex; from the root of lay. See lay. A law is that which is **laid, set or fixed**...] 1. A rule, particularly an established or permanent rule." — *Webster's 1828 Dictionary.*

God's Law and the Common Law

The Bible has always been known as God's Law, and until recently was known as "the law of the land" throughout the former British Empire. This law never changes; as no one on earth has the authority to change one word of it. If God says something is wrong, it was wrong six thousand years ago, and it is still wrong today, and it wil be wrong tomorrow. This is consistent with God's character:

"For I am the LORD, I change not;" — Malichi 3:6.

Similar, though not identical to God's Law is the common law of Britain.

Common Law: "That which derives its force and

authority from the universal consent and <u>immemorial practice</u> of the people. It has never received the sanction of the legislature, by an express act, which is the criterion by which <u>it is distinguished from the statute law</u>." — *Bouvier's Law Dictionary, 1856.*

Common law is based on the traditions of men, but cannot be radically altered because that is the nature of tradition. As long as you obeyed the Ten Commandments, the government mostly left you alone. This is in stark contrast to the intrusive and ever-changing statutes we think of as "law" today.

3
Two States

Two New Zealands

Today we are told that God's Law has been replaced by statutory law, and on the surface this certainly appears to be true. However, all law is based on precedent, so you cannot throw out a system of law without a revolution of the kind as has never occurred openly in the English speaking world. So what actually happened? If you can accept that there are two laws, maybe you are prepared to hear that there are also two New Zealands.

As this is true in most places you can freely substitute for New Zeland the name of the Country, State, Province, or other political entity you are trying to figure out.

The Nation or Country of New Zealand

We have no trouble thinking of nations in geographic terms.

Land on a beach, cross a river, or step over an imaginary line in the sand, and you can be suddenly "in" another country or nation. Once there, so we are told, we are bound to obey all their laws. If we don't like those territorial laws, the inhabitants are quick to tell us, we should find somewhere else that suits us better. The inhabitants have accepted those laws without question, and so must we. A place like New Zealand is quite easily defined geographically, so how could there possibly be more than one New Zealand?

Emergence of the Nation-State

We learned in school that the countries on the globe are "nation-states," and that this is a relatively new phenomenon in history. What we were not told is what is new about this arrangement.

Because Americans, Australians, and others call the various regions within their nation, "States," many think of a State as merely a smaller territory within a nation. As it turns out, the words "nation" and "state" mean very **different** things, and their combination into the idea of the "nation-state" may be the greatest **illusion** ever foisted upon mankind.

State: "n. 1 the existing condition or position of a person or thing." — *Concise Oxford Dictionary, Eighth edition.*

State, "government. In its most enlarged sense, it signifies a self-sufficient body of persons united together in one community…" — *Bouvier's Law Dictionary, 1856.*

State, condition of persons. If we inquire into its origin, it will be found to come from the Latin **status**, which is derived from…statio, which signifies the place where a person is located, stat, to fulfill the obligations which are imposed upon him. — *Bouvier's Law Dictionary, 1856.*

"Status" has to do to with our "relation to others."

So a state is a much more abstract concept than a nation or country. It describes the **political affiliation** of a group of people, but says nothing about their **geographic location**.

While it may make logical sense for neighbors to band together politically, it is completely unnecessary to the concept of a state. Thus you can have more than one state within the same territory, or a state can span multiple territories.

Then why is this word "State" used so often to describe a geographic entity? Enter the grand **illusion** of the nation-state.

The modern world has been organized so that political States are limited to the geographic boundaries defined by nations. Thus the laws of a particular State only apply if you are **within** its corresponding nation. But didn't the nation already have laws? Why the need to distinguish between the "nation" and the "State" if they are both within the same territory?

To answer this question we must return to the two laws.

Statute: "The written will of the legislature, solemnly expressed according to the forms prescribed in the constitution. 2. This word is used in contradistinction to the common law." — *Bouvier's Law Dictionary, 1856.*

To write these statutes, we see that there must be a constitution.

Constitution, "government. The fundamental law of the state, …" — *Bouvier's Law Dictionary, 1856.*

Next we see that a constitution is peculiar to the State, having nothing whatsoever to do with the Nation. Unlike the nations, which have been around for thousands of years, the idea of the State, and its organizational document, a constitution, is a much more recent **invention**.

"The modern idea of a constitution began to emerge after the Reformation, particularly in the works of Thomas Hobbes, John Locke, and Jean-Jacques Rousseau, who developed the notion of the **social contract**. In the social-contract view, a people agree among themselves to give up a portion of the absolute freedom of the pre-social "state of nature" in return for the security that an acknowledged government can provide.

It was John Locke's work, particularly, on the division of rights between those assigned to the government and those retained by individuals, and on the division of powers within the government, that influenced the late 18th century authors of the American Declaration of Independence, the U.S. Constitution, and the French Declaration of the Rights of Man and the Citizen." — *Encyclopedia Britannica, 2002.*

So, the State comes into being when a group of people agree to be bound by a social contract formalized in a constitution.

Out of this arrangement, statutes may be issued with much more flexibility than God's Law would ever allow. A contract only requires **mutual agreement**, so the statutes can be anything the members of the State want, and can be changed as often as the members please. If a group of thieves organize their own State and make theft legal, who could object? As long as you do not **join** their State, their peculiar "law" does not affect you.

The Law of the Land

Just like "state," the word "statute" comes from the root "status." So the State and its statutes are free-floating or relative — subject only to our relation to others.

Another maxim of law says, "The law of the land and the law of God are one; and both favor and protect the common good of the land." Just as a nation or country is tied to the land, so is God's Law, complete with the permanence this implies. As we saw from the example in Daniel, this inflexible understanding of law goes back thousands of years.

But suddenly the social-contract view provided a model whereby men had the freedom to **change** "laws" to suit their whims. All that was required to do this was to be organized politically as a "State."

However, we know from the definition of law that statutes can never actually change what is fixed. Something is **lawful** if it conforms to God's Law. So while Caesar may disagree with God, he actually lacks the authority to place his opinion above God's. All he can do through statute is to make what God says is lawful illegal or make unlawful activities **legal**. But for this trick to work, Caesar must also convince you that it is more important to do what is legal than to do only what is lawful.

Legal: "Latin *legalis*. Pertaining to the understanding, the exposition, the administration, the science and the practice of law: … Opposed to actual. "Legal" looks more to the letter, and "Lawful" to the spirit, of the law. "Legal" is more appropriate for conformity to positive rules of law; "Lawful" for accord with ethical principle. … "Legal" is the antithesis of "equitable", …" — 2 Abbott's Law Dict. 24; A Dictionary of Law, William C. Anderson, (1893).

If we look up the synonyms of "antithesis" and "equitable" we find that this last statement actually and literally says; "**Legal is the exact opposite of just and fair**." Remember this the next time someone tries to tell you something is illegal.

So while law limits Caesar's power, statutes provide Caesar with a means for poking his head into places never before imaginable.

For example, nowhere in scripture will you find the idea of a tax based on a percentage of wages. It simply is not lawful. A man's labor never belonged to Caesar. It is Caesar's statutes which make it "legal" for him to take a man's wages. Thus, without statutes Caesar could not tax any percentage of income at all!

The idea of the nation-state provides a device for overruling the Laws of God with the statutes of man and the State. This way, when the nation cannot do something **lawfully**, the State merely has to write a statute to do it **legally** instead. So today, a nation such as New Zealand will also have a mirror State operating within in it that goes by the same name.

4
Two Men

TWO MEN

There is one element missing from the redemption premis, so far: A "man on the land," in the nation, must **volunteer** into the **social contract**, making him a "citizen of the State." Otherwise Caesar's new statutes have no authority over him.

This has been accomplished so effectively today that we have no idea that there is a distinction between a "man on the land" and a "citizen of the State." There are Two types of "laws," and Two "United States," and Two "YOUs" as well.

THE LAWFUL MAN OF GOD

"What one creates, one controls" is a principle of God's Truth. Bake a cake, build a shed, or birth a baby, and it is yours, **unless** you sell it or give it away.

God created us, so He gets to control us.

We were all born within a "nation" and therefore have a "nation-ality" (*nationality*). However, the nation did not create us, so it only gets to control us to the extent that we break God's Law. As long as we behave *lawfully,* the government has little if any role to play in our lives.

This is the scriptural purpose of government:

<u>"Rulers are not a terror to good works, but to the evil</u>. *Wilt thou then not be afraid of the power? do that which is good, and thou shalt have praise of the same:*

The Hidden Truth

For he is the minister of God to thee for good. But if thou do that which is evil, be afraid; for he beareth not the sword in vain: for <u>he is the minister of God, a revenger to execute wrath upon him that doeth evil.</u>" — Romans 13:3-4.

THE ARTIFICIAL "PERSON"

For the State to have control over something, it must first create it.

The State has created a ***fictitious identity*** to mirror the living man. It offers benefits to the ***fictitious identity,*** and if the livng man accepts the benefits — **without protest** — he accepts the State's control over him, as well his fictitious strawman.

Any time the State creates an **identity document** such as an employee badge, a driver's license or a passport, it contains certain **key elements** that make it a creation of the State, and not a true identification of you.

The ***first element*** is the *name*. The name is always spelled in ALL CAPITAL LETTERS. You were never taught in school to spell your name this way; this is improper English. *In law, anything spelled contrary to the rules of English is a legal fiction.* So when you ACCEPT improper spelling, you are actually accepting an entirely new name: a name given to your mirror image strawman by the State.

The ***second element*** of the fictitious identity is the *birth date*. There are usually other numbers as well, but this is a key one. While your parents may have told you, and a birth certificate may say so, you can never testify as to the day you were born.

Perhaps you never were. It is something you can't

possibly remember or know, and therefore cannot witness to. Because of this, every time a State employee asks you what your birth date is and you tell them, they have enticed you to lie and **you perjure yourself**. **Hearsay** information is inadmissible in a court of law.

If they want your parents to testify, or to enter your birth certificate as evidence, that would be OK. However, it will **only and always** be hearsay if it comes from you. Thus, this date on an identification document is another fiction, because you will constantly be asked to verify that it is correct, and you cannot ever testify truthfully if it is or not.

So any time you see **the ALL CAPS name** and **the birth date**, you are really looking at the artificial PERSON STRAWMAN.

Most State benefits are only available to him, and he is the actual "citizen" of the State. Things are deliberately structured this way to get the lawful Christian man to **volunteer** to identify himself as the artificial PERSON instead, and therefore as being a jurisdictional subject of the State.

ARE YOU REALLY A "PERSON"?

In this day of gender sensitivity, we have been carefully taught to replace sexist words like "man" with the supposed synonym "person." However, when we admit to being a "person" in law, we are declaring that we are something that we are not — something very different from a lawful woman or man. The word "person" comes from the Latin "persona," meaning "an actor's mask." Like your "person-ality" (*personality*), your "person" may be what others see, but it is not

The Hidden Truth

you at all.

"This word 'person' and its scope and bearing in the law, involving as it does **legal fictions** and also **apparently** natural beings, it is difficult to understand, — but it is absolutely necessary to grasp, at whatever cost, a true and proper understanding of the word in all the phases of its proper use. A "person" is here not a physical or individual person, but the **status** or condition with which he is invested. The law of persons is the law of **status** or condition." — *American Law and Procedure, Vol 13, page 137, 1910.*

So again we see that whether or not we are PERSONS under the STATUTES of the State, all comes back to the question of our **status**. It has nothing to do with law at all.

IDEM SONANS: [adj.] "Sounding the same. 2. In pleadings, when a name that is material to state is wrongly spelled, yet if it be *idem sonans* with that which is proved it is sufficient, as Segrave for Seagrave." — *Bouvier's Law Dictionary, 1856.*

When spoken out loud, your REAL name and the ALL CAPS name sound exactly the same. Yet in writing they are easy to distinguish. Not surprisingly, it is just as easy to distinguish between the nation and the State.

THE "STATE OF THE UNITED STATES" IS THE FICTION

Thus, the STATE that is the counterpart to the NATION named the United States is the "nation-state" called the UNITED STATES. This appears correctly on printed documents. People are not so careful when hand-writing these names, as they seldom know that there is a difference between the two. Often, a government official will work for both the nation and the State, and his titles will reflect this:

1. The United States Treasury Secretary, and

2. THE SECRETARY OF THE TREASURY <u>OF</u> THE UNITED STATES. Two distinct titles. [The word "of" means, "belonging to."]

This also reveals two distinct departments, one department for the nation, and another department for the State:

1.1. The United States Treasury <u>for</u> the United States, and 1.2. THE TREASURY <u>OF</u> THE UNITED STATES.

2.1. The Constitution <u>for</u> the United States, and 2.2. THE CONSTITUTION <u>OF</u> THE UNITED STATES.

Now we can look at the Two laws, the two United States, and the Two men, and see that there is an exact correspondence, and an initial answer to the question posed by the titles of these reports:

The Things That Are God's: The real...

1. Nation: New Zeland; A piece of Land; like the United States of America.
2. God's Law: Fixed; The law of the land; Lawful.
3. Lawful Man of God: A Bondman of Christ; Lawful Christian name; No numbers; Owned and controlled by God.
4. Determined by LAW: Are you doing good or evil?

The Things That Are Caesar's: Legal fictions...

1. State: NEW ZELAND; A Corporation; like the UNITED STATES.

2. Statutory "law": Codes; Rules and Regulations; Statutes; Arbitrary: Based on the whims of men; legal

3. Artificial PERSON/STRAWMAN: A Citizen ALL CAPS name & birth date; Owned and controlled by the State, unless commercially redeemed

4. Determined by Status: Are you under Contract? or are you free?

Simply being within the geographic boundaries of the nation is not sufficient to make you subject to the statutes of the State. Yet the State has been so successful in getting us all to *volunteer* into its scheme that you probably don't know anyone for whom this makes a practical difference.

What the rest of these reports will show is why it is crucial to understand the distinction, and to *"choose you this day whom ye will serve ..."* — Joshua 24:15.

5
Divine Right of Kings

When we search out the origins of this modern governmental dichotomy, we find it rooted in Two very different views of the source of rightful authority. The **established** view was that all authority flows from God Himself, and that the only scriptural form of government is a **theocracy,** presided over by God himself. Thus, the people were subject to a king's authority so long as the king was subject to God's authority. This view survives today in governmental oath's of office.

The Queen of England is sworn to uphold the laws of God and the proclamation of the gospel. In her coronation ceremony, this oath was immediately followed by the presentation of the Holy Scriptures, lest there be any doubt as to what laws and gospel these referred to.

In The United States, and no doubt in the rest of the British Commonwealth, the police and judges are sworn to serve the Queen, as she is still the head of the nation. Thus the people are to obey the police and judges because they are under a lawful chain of authority traceable back to God Himself.

CONSENT OF THE GOVERNED

But along with the Reformation came a **competing** idea of how to set up a legitimate form of government. The thought was that this new form would be superior to the old, since it would address the abuses that were so prevalent among Kings who did not take God's authority over them seriously enough. Instead of appealing to the *scriptures* for its authority, this new form of government would be created by **a group of men** simply agreeing on how they wanted to be governed.

This new thinking would finally come to full bloom in the form of the American Declaration of Independence. In part:

"We hold these Truths to be self-evident, that all Men are created equal, that they are endowed by their Creator with certain unalienable Rights, that among these are Life, Liberty and the Pursuit of Happiness. That to <u>secure these Rights, Governments are instituted</u> among Men, <u>deriving their just Powers from the Consent of the Governed</u>. That whenever any Form of Government becomes destructive of these Ends, <u>it is the Right of the People to alter or to abolish it, and to institute new Government</u>, laying its Foundation on such Principles, and organizing its Powers in such Forms, <u>as to them shall seem most likely</u> to effect their Safety and Happiness."

Several things were achieved with this universally praised but divisive document. **First,** it laid all the blame for the colonies' problems at the foot of King George, dealing a major blow to the already embattled concept of monarchy. **Second,** it stated the **social-contract** view as the basis for the authority of the new government. While the Creator is given credit for unalienable Rights, the authority to institute, alter, or abolish government rests solely with "the People" and is guided by nothing more than their fickle opinion of what seems best at the time. **Finally,** *and very significantly,* the Declaration created a new political entity,

the State, that would obscure the meaning of the word "state" for generations to come.

A new nation was born, consisting supposedly of thirteen geographic subdivisions called "States," and to burn this into the mind of every man, the new nation would be called **the united "States" of America**. What had really been created for the first time in history was **a political entity** independent of the biblical authority structure of previous nations. This was to be the new model for the world as evidenced by the unfolding of **the nation-state** across the entire globe, and its accompanying organizational document, **a divisive constitution**.

An interesting note is that in New Zeland the people are told that they do NOT have a constitution. However, a peek into the Preamble of the Australian Constitution shows:

6. "The Commonwealth" shall mean the Commonwealth of Australia as established under this Act. "The States" shall mean such of the colonies of New South Wales, New Zeland, Queensland, Tasmania, Victoria, Western Australia, and South Australia, …

This makes it clear why people from either country may freely live and work in the other, and the currencies are identical shapes and sizes, among other "coincidences." *Australia and New Zeland are separate nations but* **the same federated State**. Ponder that one for a while. Read between the lines.

6
Constitutional Freedoms

The second greatest illusion ever foisted upon mankind is the idea that a constitution is the means of securing liberties. To sell this new idea regarding government required a **mythology** that it was an improvement on all previous forms. America, we were told, was to be a model of freedom for the rest of the world. In other words, once government **based on the whims of men** (*and not the Will of God*) was accepted, it could be sold wholesale to everyone else on the planet.

What they failed to tell anyone was the divisive hook: "**a constitution creates <u>constitutors</u>.**"

CONSTITUTOR: "Civil law. He who promises by a <u>simple pact</u> to pay the <u>debt of another</u>; and this is <u>always a principal obligation</u>." — *Bouvier's Law Dictionary, 1856.*

If we turn to Article Six of the United States Constitution we find:

"All Debts contracted and Engagements entered into, before the Adoption of this Constitution, shall be as valid against the United States under this Constitution, as under the Confederation."

So the State requires a constitution and a constitution requires a debt to be paid. **Pay off the debt, and the State ceases to exist!**

The existence of all modern governments is predicated on the fact that their citizens have become

"**SURETY**" for someone else's debt, and this debt can never be repaid.

"He that is surety for a stranger shall smart for it: and he that hateth suretiship is sure." — Proverbs 11:15.

No matter what country you are in, one reality that makes news on a regular basis is the ever-growing national debt (*federal debt*). Did you ever wonder who actually has the money lying around to make such enormous loans? Is there some nation out there that is super-rich, loaning all their money to the rest of the world?

In fact, all the so-called "rich" nations are heavily in debt, and bankrupt, so just where does all this debt/money come from?

Enter the **illusion** of modern fractional reserve banking. Today central banks are allowed to issue fictitious currencies backed by nothing of value, and in turn to collect interest on that "money" they creat out of nothing but thin air. They loan this "money" to the government, and we get to pay it back, plus interest, by the very real sweat of our brow. Pretty neat, huh? Who says money doesn't grow upon "trees"?

The "laws" that allow the bankers to play such a trick can only be statutory, for this is completely against God's Law. So for the game to work, those paying the debt must all be **members of a State**, not merely a nation. This creates the necessity of a constitution to turn men into "citizens," or "constitutors" of that created State. Then they are bound by the statutes written for the purpose of collecting this debt.

What is at first surprising is just how alike the statutes are in distant countries, like Australia, and the United States, for example.

However, once you learn that the statutes are written by the same group of attorneys working for the Crown's bankers who loaned the "money" to both nations, it makes perfect sense. Local legislatures seldom do more than make minor cosmetic changes before "rubber-stamping" these statutes into "law."

DROWNING IN DEBT

Though nations are tied to God's Law, and modern law is still dependent upon it for precedence, today we are told in courtrooms that God's Law is irrelevant. How can this be so? Because once a debt is established, it becomes a means of control just as scripture says.

"The rich ruleth over the poor, and <u>the borrower is servant to the lender</u>." — *Proverbs 22:7.*

Since it is called the "<u>national</u>" debt, we know that it is the <u>nation</u>, not the State that is in debt. At one time or another every nation has defaulted on its debt, forcing it to declare bankruptcy. Bankruptcy severely undermines the nation's laws.

BANKRUPTCY: "The state or condition of a bankrupt. 2. <u>Bankrupt laws are an encroachment upon the common law</u>." — *Bouvier's Law Dictionary, 1856.*

BANKRUPT: "Again, the bankrupt laws are intended mainly <u>to secure creditors</u> from waste, extravagance, and mismanagement, <u>by seizing property</u> out of the hands of the debtors, <u>and placing it in the custody of the law</u>." — *Bouvier's Law Dictionary, 1856.*

When a nation declares bankruptcy, all its assets are seized and managed by another entity that is charged with using those assets to pay the debt.

What are the assets of a nation? The three principle ones are its <u>land</u>, its **vehicles**, and its **people**!

All titles to land and vehicles, along with all birth certificates are turned over to the entity managing the bankruptcy. But what entity is that? Conveniently it was already sitting there, complete with a form of "law," ready to take custody of the property within. It is **the State**, created by debt, and eager for a greater role in **managing** and **collecting** that debt!

And so, **the statutes** that manage the bankruptcy **override the laws** of the bankrupt nation.

7
Two Men, Revisited

But simply pledging birth certificates is insufficient to turn free men into debtor/slaves without their consent. This is accomplished more subtly, for several reasons. The most significant reason for hiding what is going on is that **"the most productive slaves are slaves who <u>believe</u> they are free."**

So you continue the *propaganda* about freedom in the now bankrupt nation because it makes debt collection far easier.

In all likelihood, your name is spelled properly on your birth certificate. If you immigrate to The United States, the visa will also be issued in your real name. This seems quite odd, especially as it gets placed within the pages of a Passport that has only the ALL CAPS name in it.

Immigration, it turns out, is really transferring yourself as an asset from one nation to another, and it will be **the State of the UNITED STATES**, not **the nation of the United States of America** that considers you of sufficient value to be accepted as one of theirs, for bankruptcy collection and settlement purposes. Once here, you will be promptly turned over to the State of the UNITED STATES for management, and all other documents will be issued only to your artificial PERSON/STRAWMAN.

So if you look on the title to your house or vehicle, you will see that it has the ALL CAPS name on it, meaning it is not really owned by you at all, but by the creditors of the bankrupt, corporate UNITED STATES. The artificial PERSON/STRAWMAN is a fiction, and a fictitious entity CANNOT own anything.

8
Two Laws, Revisited

As a bondservant of Christ, you are obliged at all times to obey God's Law. However, you cannot leave your house without the State pushing contracts and benefits at you for your acceptance. The moment you sign a form or accept a benefit, you are now under contract with the State and are identified as one of their artificial PERSONS. As such you are bound by all their debt collection contracts, known as **"statutory laws."** These are not true "laws," as they are ever-changing, and because they are contracts there is no limit to their terms. You are **presumed** to have agreed to whatever those terms are when you **voluntarily** agreed to be under contract. So if those terms contradict your fundamental freedoms, it is **presumed** that you willingly gave them away.

Interestingly, the same Article Six of the United States Constitution where the debts are affirmed is also where religious tests for public office are forbidden.

This was another novation in law masquerading as a "freedom." Previously it was assumed that those administering the laws of the nation (God's Law) were fellow believers in Christ who upheld God's Law privately as well as publicly. Removing this requirement paved the way for the "secular" courts we have today.

These courts get to uphold statutes that are contrary to God's Law, as the officers of the court are not bound publicly or privately to uphold God's Law. So while God's Law can never be replaced as the law of the land, it is being treated as irrelevant today.

9
Four Laws

To understand what takes place in a modern court it is necessary to expand our Two categories of law to Four. First we will look at **the laws of the nation**. The Queen of England has sworn an oath to uphold "the laws of God" and "the laws of the Commonwealth."

No one can swear to do two contradictory actions at the same time, so these two laws cannot be in conflict with each other. What this means is that the "laws of Commonwealth" are a practical outworking of the "laws of God." They are synonymous as **the law of the land.**

In front of a judge this will have great significance, for if you mention the laws of God he will counter that he is sworn to uphold **the laws of the UNITED STATES** — and he is.

You will now be in his court under a charge of violating a **statute of the UNITED STATES** not a **law of the United States of America**, but he hopes you will not know the difference between the two. His statutes need the legitimacy of being thought of as "law" and he doesn't want you to know that he is violating his own oath of office.

Should you seek to separate yourself from contractual relationships with the statutes of the UNITED STATES, you will soon discover a clear double-standard within those statutes.

While the police and judges of the UNITED STATES are very eager to obtain rigid compliance from you to their statutes, they do not feel nearly the same urgency to obey their statutes themselves.

In a small place like New Zeland, with no division of powers within the government, this truly makes them "a law unto themselves." But who can blame them for using their own contracts to their advantage? After all, any contractual relationship is **voluntary,** right? But for the system to work they must convince you that it is **NOT voluntary,** but compelled.

Another side to the double-standard is just who the law enforcers are. Most judges and many police are members of the Masonic order. They swear other oaths in contradiction to their oath of office, such as to never convict any member of their order of any crime less serious than treason or murder. This means that the statutes they will throw you behind bars for, they do not apply to themselves. So while they huff and puff about how important their statutory "law" is, statutory "law" is really "two" laws, one for us and another for them.

Now we can see the breakdown of the four laws:

Law
1. God's Law: Law of the Land.
2. Laws of New Zeland: Consistent with God's Law; The Queen, police, and judges are bound to uphold.
Binding on: All men within the Nation.
Source of Authority: Traceable back to God.
Foundational Document: Holy Scripture.

Debt Collection Rules
3. Statutes of NEW ZELAND: As applied to the general public.

4. Statutes of New Zeland: As applied to its own employees, police and judges enforce.
Binding on: Only those under Contract.
Source of Authority: Consent of the Governed.
Foundational Document: A Constitution.

10
Three United States

The final piece of the puzzle of modern government is that there is yet another United States. It appears on many documents under the name "**US**" with no punctuation. Were it punctuated, it would merely be an abbreviation for one of the other two United States, though we would have no way of knowing which one. But **"US"** is a third entity altogether.

In the United States there are also two-letter designations for each State, and this gives us a clue as to what **US** really is. **ME** is not the lawful Maine Republic, it is the debt collection agency of MAINE, which is an enclave of the United States Federal government within Maine. So anyone who admits to being "in" **ME** is actually placing themselves under the jurisdiction of the Federal government.

Most Americans accept mail delivered to their house with only the two-letter designation, and thus unwittingly give the Federal government authority over them that it would not normally have, unless rebutted. This is one way we make ourselves "subject" to statutes of the Federal Income Tax.

Should you be approved as an immigrant to the United States, you will receive a visa granting you the right to "live and work in the **US**." There will be plenty of room on the visa to spell The United States out in full, leaving you to wonder why they apparently couldn't be bothered to do so. However, we already have a number of clues that tell us this is no accident.

First, does government have the lawful (*i.e. God-given*) authority to decide who can or cannot inhabit a nation and work there? The fact that the visa does not grant the right to live and work in "The United States" is actually a confession that the government has no such authority.

Second, we know that MAINE is a State within the nation the United States, and that their statutes are written by the same people who wrote the statutes of the UNITED STATES. So in all likelihood the Income Tax in MAINE is really a statute of the federal UNITED STATES, as opposed to a statute of Maine. Thus, if they want to tax your wages, it is critical that they get you to **"accept"** the privilege of living, and especially working, within the Federal jurisdiction known as the **US**.

Finally, since it violates the rules of written English, we know that the **US** is another legal fiction, not a lawful government. So its main purpose is simply to bind us with even more debt collection statutes.

This is just one example of how the government fools us into giving them authority over us. First, they make a claim to have a power they do not lawfully have, such as telling you where you may or may not work. Then, once you believe that you no longer have this God-given freedom (*the ability to support your family*), they offer you a government-granted **privilege, or benefit,** in its place. As soon as you ask for and **"accept"** this benefit, *without protest,* you are now under their control. So when you present your visa to an employer as "proof" that you are allowed to work for him, you also give him the rightful authority to take a portion of your wages and send it to the government. You have just taken what is God's (*and what God has freely given to you*) and rendered it to Caesar.

11
Unlimited Power To Contract

If we were to list all the God-given freedoms that we have voluntarily **"exchanged"** for inferior government privileges, we would fill a depressing number of pages.

We have been trapped by our own ignorance of the law, despite being told early in life that **"ignorance of the law is no excuse."**

Once we start doing business with Caesar, willingly giving him what is God's, we find ourselves locked into a web of detrimental PRESUMPTIVE and EXPRESS contracts.

A key point to understand is that there are absolutely no limits in law to what two parties can agree to by contract, as long as it does not involve harming a third party. So if you agree to give all your property to another party, or to be treated however that party may deem best, there is nothing in law to which you can appeal, should you later discover you've been had.

Caesar's modern State is just such a contractual relationship, with one key difference: we were never told we were **contracting** our God-given freedoms away as an effect of fraud.

First, it is an all or nothing contract. If you agree to one part, you agree to the whole thing. So Christians who think they should go along with the statutes of the State, out of obedience to scripture, are in fact giving legitimacy to ALL the godless actions of the State.

We were told that we had no choice but to accept

the ALL because "it's the law." However, we now see that this is not "the Law" at all. But simply a contractual relationship. And, as such, the contract can be terminated.

Second, this contract, at its root, involves the payment of debts we never agreed to. We have been sold into bondage by fraud, and unless something changes we will sell our children and grandchildren into this same ever worsening bondage, for "a mess of pottage."

Third, the scriptural solution is to *"come out of her, my people."* (*Revelation 18:4; II Corinthians 6:17*).

This does not mean coming out of the nation or violating its laws. These laws are still consistent with the Law of God and are what scripture refers to when telling us to obey legitimate earthly authority. However, when we obey judges and police who are sworn to uphold legitimate **laws,** but are instead enforcing a separate and contradictory set of **statutes**, we become **party** to their evil, in that we neither uphold legitimate law, nor honor God. We devote our energies to obeying the whims of men, which change almost over night and grow increasingly depraved. It is the statutory, contract law of the State that we must stop trying to "fix," but instead "reject" and no longer uphold.

12
Mark of the Beast

Now that you understand the structure of modern law, you are prepared to see how perfectly scripture described it thousands of years in advance. Most Christians are waiting for the day when a computer chip will be implanted in their forehead or in their hand. At that time they will make a decision to accept it or reject it. What they do not realize is the fact that they have already accepted the mark of the beast.

"And he causeth all, both small and great, rich and poor, free and bond, to receive a mark <u>in their right hand</u>, or <u>in their foreheads</u>: And that no man might buy or sell, save he that had <u>the mark</u>, or <u>the name</u> of the beast, or <u>the number</u> of his name."
— Revelation 13:16-17.

First note that there is not just a MARK, but also a NAME and a NUMBER.

What does the State always need from you? The artificial PERSON NAME and birth date, or other NUMBER such as a Social Security Number. We have to love the honesty of the Canadians who call it a Social Insurance Number, or SIN, instead of a SSN.

We cannot do business with the State without these three things, nor can we open a bank account or access other conveniences of modern society without them. Each year it becomes more challenging to buy and sell without the MARK, the NAME, or the NUMBER of the beast.

But the MARK is the real kicker, and it has been sitting there in scripture all along.

"And it shall be for a sign unto thee <u>upon thine hand</u>, and for a memorial <u>between thine eyes</u>, that <u>God's law</u> may be in thy mouth."— Exodus 13:9.

This is repeated in one of the most famous passages of the Old Testament:

"Hear, O Israel: The LORD our God is one LORD: And thou shalt love the LORD thy God with all thine heart, and with all thy soul, and with all thy might. And these words, which I command thee this day, shall be in thine heart: And thou shalt teach them diligently unto thy children, and shalt talk of them when thou sittest in thine house, and when thou walkest by the way, and when thou liest down, and when thou risest up. And thou shalt bind them for a <u>sign upon thine hand</u>, and they shall be as <u>frontlets between thine eyes</u>. And thou shalt write them upon the posts of thy house, and on thy gates." — Deuteronomy 6:4-9.

What is supposed to already be in our hand and in our forehead (*between thine eyes*)? God's Law!

If God's Law is there, how could the beast's counterfeit MARK take its place? The modern church has neglected God's Law in the name of being **"not under law, but under grace."** In its place we have accepted the beast's **statute law** as his **MARK**. Because people no longer think of Law as something "fixed" or unchanging, the church misses the blessing of having an unchanging Law to follow, and accepts in its place the burden of ever-changing statutes.

"Grace" is taught as being the opposite of Law, when the true biblical opposite of Law is "iniquity" — or lawlessness. How many Christians, "under grace" are, in fact, living "in iniquity?"

The failure to understand leads the church to teach that obedience to ever-changing statutes is what Peter and Paul had in mind when they tell us to submit to earthy authorities. Yet these **statutes** are contradictory to and a replacement for the **Law of God**. This is precisely what Daniel saw several millennia ago while in Babylon:

"Thus he said, The fourth beast shall be the fourth kingdom upon earth, which shall be diverse from all kingdoms, and shall <u>devour the whole earth</u>, and shall tread it down, and <u>break it in pieces</u>. And he shall speak great words against the most High, and shall <u>wear out the saints</u> of the most High, and think to <u>change times and laws</u>: and they shall be given into his hand until a time and times and the dividing of time." — Daniel 7:23, 25.

The modern church has already embraced the MARK, the NAME, and the NUMBER of the beast, and continues to tell its members to do so, as good Christians. In the name of obedience to God, most are busily and unknowingly rendering unto Caesar the things that rightfully should be rendered unto God.

Caesar has usurped God's authority, but his kingdom is built with our consent, by using legal fictions in our behalf. Caesar's authority over us is imaginary. We do not have to render ourselves unto him, unless we believe that we belong to him.

Commercial Redemption is also a part of God's Plan.

13
The Conversion

There is no telling when **the conversion** took place but one of the major factors was the incorporation of the UNITED STATES in 1871 with the final act occurring in 1878. The UNITED STATES is not the united States of the Union; it is a separate entity.

From the Statutes at Large it looked like this was only the incorporation of the District of Columbia but in the final act there is the phrase, "District of Columbia **or** United States" making these two phrases interchangeable, allowing the UNITED STATES to operate as a private corporation conducting business from that time on.

The *de facto* "government" operating in this country today as a Democracy is not the *de jure* Republic created by the Constitution; it's a for-profit corporation operating in Commerce. Every transaction of the UNITED STATES is a commercial transaction by fictions at law.

A fiction at law, or legal fiction, is an artificially created entity only contemplated in law. In other words, it is not real except in the eyes of law written by man.

Legal fictions are the opposite of natural entities such as people. A created legal fiction is endowed by the law to have privileges that resemble the rights that people have, such as the right to hold property and to sue.

The most common legal fictions are corporations and trusts. These have been around for some time with their main purpose being to limit the liability of the people holding the corporation or trust, allowing them to be responsible for their actions only as a select group instead of individually.

Legal fictions are not compatible with common law, the law this country was founded upon. In common law each one is responsible for his own actions and is held accountable and responsible for anything he does right or wrong.

In 1933 the Governors of all the States met to discuss the state of emergency declared by President Franklin Delano Roosevelt based on the bankruptcy of the UNITED STATES, to support the new commercial process that was being established to administer the bankruptcy.

The state governments made a pledge to the UNITED STATES to fund the bankruptcy. The governors pledged the assets and energy of the people of the states to support the "government" and secure the corporate, national debt. But there was a problem. The governors could only speak for the people in their public capacity. They could not pledge private, living, human beings or private property. It was therefore necessary to create a bridge (*a connecting link*) between the living people and the creditors of the bankruptcy. The solution was to create Strawmen to stand in the place of the people themselves.

In making the pledge, the Governors agreed to register the Birth Records of the people with the U.S. Department of Commerce. The Birth Record is the Security instrument (*collateral*) that backs the pledge.

The legal fiction was created by stating its name on a Birth Certificate and writing it in all capital letters, the designation for a legal fiction. Then because of the pledge, YOU were determined to be the representative and surety (*co-signer*) for the legal fiction, your mirror image, fictitious strawman.

Surety means: "The one who is responsible to pay."

Therefore, when the "government" or any corporation uses any procedure they are using it in reference to the legal fiction which they want you to think is YOU, but when your name is written in all capital letters, IT IS NOT YOUR NAME! It's the name of a legal fiction (*your ens legis strawman*), an entirely separate entity.

A living human being cannot be a legal fiction and a legal fiction cannot be a living human being. One is real or natural; the other is created by a presumption of law.

Whenever a government agency (*such as court*) determines liability, it's the liability of the fictional strawman because everything is done in Commerce, not in the real world. You are presumed, because of the governors' pledge, to be the surety for your Strawman so you must pay the liability.

The Strawman is not you. The Strawman is owned and controlled by the State because he has been pledged to the State. In practical application, the doctrine of the Strawman gives the real man the ability to exist with all his rights secured by the Constitution. To reach that position you must **pay back the pledge** and **redeem the collateral** that has been pawned.

Many people are using **CPR** — the Commercial Process of Redemption — to pay the pledge and redeem their Strawman from the pledge. This wrests the Strawman from government control and makes you the beneficiary of your *ens legis* strawman.

The Strawman is a **"transmitting utility."** Think of him as a pipeline through which goods and services pass from a main supply to customers such as yourself, like a gas line or water line to your house.

The creditors of the U.S. bankruptcy have the goods and services under their control. They cannot deal with living human beings because they are not the real government, they are only private corporations of one and can only do business with other artificial entities. If they deal with real people their fiction would disintegrate and they would be **exposed** for the illusion that they are, and be committing **Treason.**

So in today's world, for a real living human being to get the things he needs, he must have an intermediate, a "go-between," a Strawman, **a "transmitting utility"** that exists in the artificial world. Your relationship with your Strawman is the Key.

Before your Strawman is redeemed the government holds "him" as a pledge for its federal debts. The government owns and controls the Strawman. Everything that passes through the **"pipeline"** belongs to the government and anyone making use of those things is presumed to be the **surety** for the Strawman.

Once you pay back the pledge, your Strawman is redeemed from government control and you become the creditor of your Strawman because your Strawman is then in debt to you, instead of to the government.

This creditor/debtor relationship is documented by stating your claim on a UCC-1 Financing Statement filed in the public record with your Secretary of State.

Since you are now the creditor of your **pipeline/ strawman** you have an interest in everything that passes through the pipe. You are no longer presumed to be the surety of your Strawman, you are his **beneficiary** instead.

What this does for you is demonstrated in the movie *Amistad.* In *Amistad,* people from a village in Africa were taken prisoner as slaves, transported across the ocean until they finally ended up in the United States.

During the first part of their trip they were taken to a slave trading station where they were sold to slave traders in Portugal. The slave traders were issued a Bill of Sale for the **"Merchandise"** that listed the names and number of the slaves they had sold. During the trip, supplies became scarce and fifty slaves were thrown overboard to their death. Records were altered to reflect the difference in the weights of cargo and **the original records were hidden** aboard the Amistad.

The Africans managed to secure control of the ship and kill most of the crew, but were **tricked** by two surviving crew members **to sail into American waters.** The Africans were taken prisoners and charged with piracy and murder for the crew member deaths.

The first day of the court case the Bailiff called the case and read the government's charges against the Africans. And a series of other claims were made.

A second claim was made by two commissioned officers **as private citizens** who claimed the Africans and the Ship. They showed a **Salvage Title** in support their claim based on their right to salvage. These were the two crew members who were not killed who tricked the Africans into sailing into American waters.

A third claim was made by men who claimed they purchased the slaves in Portugal. They claimed that the slaves were their property and presented a Warehouse Receipt to prove their claim.

A fourth claim was made by men who were businessmen and bankers. These men were interested in promoting anti-slavery and filed a Habeas Corpus (*"produce the body"*) action for the release of the Africans to freedom.

When there is a claim filed against a Strawman, **his beneficiary** — the real, flesh and blood man — **can file a claim against the Strawman too.** He is a non-party to the suit — a third party intervenor — who has a **security interest** in the Strawman as well, the property being sued. He comes into court with his **Superior Title** to the Strawman, his UCC-1 Financing Statement/Security Contract.

The Secured Party's position is: "It matters not what you do to my Strawman, but before you take anything from him **my superior claim has to be settled first** because he owes me first.

This is the **remedy** that is available to you, the real man, the creditor of your government created Strawman.

14
The Strawman

When you were born your future productive energy was pledged to the State via your Birth Certificate that certified a bond that the State sold on the open market to fund the UNITED STATES and its interest on the National Debt. The purchaser of that bond is the Secured Party who owns the profits of your future energy output. That energy is measured in money-credits (FRNs).

The bond holder essentially owns the results of everything you do. Each person has a government created Strawman that represents this energy output, his *nom de guerre* Strawman.

If a Redemptor (*a redeemed John Doe)* gets a Summons addressed to "JOHN DOE" that summons is not addressed to him. His name is not spelled with all capital letters, therefore he was sent that Summons by mistake.

JOHN DOE is different from John Doe. JOHN DOE is not you, he is your mirror-image fiction, your government created Strawman. Every man, woman, and child has a mirror-image, fictional Strawman.

When you sign your name to any document you are co-signing for your Strawman and pledging the Title to "his" property to the corporate UNITED STATES and its common stock holders, not to you.

CPR — the Commercial Process of Redemption — gives you a way to benefit by taking control of your Strawman. Once you **employ** your Strawman you own the rights and titles to the property that "he" acquires, and a whole lot more.

The government holds the title to your Strawman by **presumption**. And when you rebut the presumption you regain ownership of your Strawman. You become a Sovereign instead of a slave. The government loses its commercial hold on you, and you gain **"standing"** at law.

Sovereigns are masters of all of they now own. They are independent of all laws, taxes, regulations, ordinances and zoning restrictions. Sovereigns are no longer citizens of the corporate UNITED STATES **Democracy**. They are citizens of the united States **Republic** instead.

The only court that can have jurisdiction over a Sovereign is a common law court, but such courts no longer exist. A Sovereign cannot be arrested for a victimless crime; such as not wearing seatbelts when you drive. Sovereigns have other benefits to boot.

All claims are brought against your Strawman who is **presumed** to be acting in your behalf.

Because you are unaware of their presumptive claims, their claims are held as truth under commercial law. All patriot failures in court are thus explained. Most patriots are unaware of the Strawman, and do not have control of their's. They do not "rebut the error and declare the truth."

TAKING BACK YOUR STRAWMAN

There are two sides to the government. A **private** side and a **public** side. The value of your Strawman's pledge is posted on the **public, debtor side** of a double-entry account and you need to move this value over to the **private, creditor side** of the account because that side has priority under the Democracy of military, martial law.

You take back your Strawman by using the value of your **Birth Certificate** to pay-off your pledge by sending a **Bill of Exchange** and a **Charge-off Letter** to the Secretary of Treasury of the UNITED STATES, with a **UCC Financing Statement/private, Security Agreement** filed with your Secretary of State.

This redeems you from the public, debtor side of the government account and places you on the private, creditor side instead. You then can own property via the Strawman that now belongs to you, as your private employee.

Not only do you now own directly what your Strawman owns, you are now the **controller** of your Strawman and his trade name. Your name is now your **credit** instead of theirs. If any person uses your name or your Strawman's name without your permission, *after being notified,* they violate the laws of "slander of credit" — a federal, securities offense.

In essence, you becomes a bank because you are attempting to collect **the security interest** underlying your Birth Certificate, your presumptive contract with the federal UNITED STATES. A banker has the capacity to create a Bill of Exchange to draw upon the public debt payable to your Strawman's credtior who is now you.

The Bond certified by your Birth Certificate was valued at $630,000 dollars in 1936. It is now thought to be valued at $1,000,000 dollars in **real money** not fake FRNs. And it has been earning interest for the government ever since you were born; a fantastic unknown sum.

After you redeem your Strawman, you can use **CPR** (*the commercial process of Redemption*) to discharge public debts with **private credit** in a tax and levy exempt mode by opening a private UCC Contract Trust Account (CTA) that you can utilize to discharge various public debts.

When you become the **"holder in due course"** of your Strawman you became his **"creditor"** and the federal government — not you — becomes responsible for any claims made against him.

If your Strawman gets a traffic ticket, you can have the government pay the fine, since the government is now the **"surety"** for your Strawman instead of you. The government is now liable for all public debts, fines and judgments incurred in and against your Strawman's name.

You can **"accept for value"** (A4V) any presentment made against your Strawman.

By this action you are notifying the presenter that he owes YOU the amount of his claim, since you now hold the title to the money the presenter has offered to you in presenting a charge against your Strawman, since you are now the **beneficiary** of your Strawman.

The presenter, however, cannot release the legal title to these public funds to you because the public side is bankrupt and owns nothing by legal title. This is an advantage you can use to your benefit.

When the presenter does not produce the title to these funds within 72 hours (*which he cannot do*), **or withdraw his charge,** a condition of dishonor occurs. You can then do a "Banker's Acceptance" of the dishonored contract. You can draw up a Bill of Exchange, and deposit it in your UCC CTA via the private capacity of the Secretary of the Treasury of the UNITED STATES.

The Secretary of the Treasury becomes the correspondent bank of your UCC Contract Trust Account who keeps an account balance in your name under you EIN or Contract Trust Account Number (CTAN).

Once the Secretary of the Treasury has established a private UCC CTA for you, you can order him to release the **private side funds** from your UCC Contract Trust Account to meet public claims presented against your Strawman. You do this with an **Order** and a UCC **Partial Release Statement** filed with the Secretary of State. In this way you are given the right to **"discharge"** any public liabilities that your Strawman might incur.

To redeem ownership of your Strawman, you must **register** your Strawman with your Secretary of State, and with your County Recorder too if real property is involved. Secretaries of State are centralized repositories for these declarations and County Recorders hold the real estate records of the local community.

THE UCC FINANCING STATEMENT

The debtor and the secured party are listed on this UCC-1 Form. This shows that the debtor owes money to the creditor; your strawman owes money to you.

When a debt is **charged** against your Strawman you can **discharge** it with a Bankers Acceptance and cancel out the debt. This lowers the National Debt because the National Debt is owed to you.

In other words: When the liability for the debt is placed against your Strawman you can **"accept it for**

value" and **offset it** with a Banker's Acceptance Order to your UCC CTA, and that part of the National Debt is discharged as a quid pro quo exchange.

This process is called **"Acceptance for Value"** and the Commercial Process of Redemption (**CPR**) is referred to as the "Acceptance for Value Process" (**AVP**). You can **"accept for value"** any public charge or claim that is presented to your Strawman: a traffic ticket; a court summons; an IRS claim; etc. Place the value upon the document and order the Secretary of the Treasury to adjust your private UCC Contract Account, accordingly.

HOW DID THIS HAPPEN?

As part of the reorganization of the United States under Chapter 11 Bankruptcy in 1933, the federal government created a fictitious "person" (*corporation*) called the federal UNITED STATES.

Legal fictions can create legal fictions. So the federal government created a **fictitious "person"** to represent each of the several States named after each State. Once this was done the entire process was established.

All areas of government, including courts of purported law, are currently authorized by and operating as **fictitious "persons."**

Courts in the United States can only recognize other legal **fictitious "persons."** This is why your lawful name is never found in their court records. It is mirrored by the fictitious person, your Strawman.

Jurisdiction in fictitious courts is only with other **fictitious "persons."** The only jurisdiction a lawful being can be subjected to is a common law (*constitu-*

tional) court, but common law courts no longer exist. Only legal law courts exist in America today.

The purpose of the government's use of proper names written in full caps is now revealed. The only way to counter this system of deception is for lawful men to **stop responding for the fictitious name** that the State has given to their Strawmen.

Every document issued by the government is addressed to the **fictitious "person"** written in full caps. Lawful Americans must insist that they are NOT the **"legal fiction"** that the government says they are, and take control of the their Strawman by redeeming and using their lawful Christian name.

IN SUMMATION

Who is the all caps person JOHN SMITH? He is the **legal fiction** that the government created to take the place of the real being John James Smith.

The government has subverted your Christian birthright (*your lawful Christian name*) by the **legal fiction** (*your Strawman*) it created to take your place in commerce.

If the lawful Christian answers as the legal person, the two are presumed to be conjoined. But when the lawful Christian claims his lawful right and takes possession of his government created Strawman, the two are no longer conjoined but are two separate entities, and the lawful Christian's name is thereby redeemed. Herein lies the Remedy: **"Separation of Strawman and State."**

15
Manmade v. Real

"Judge not according to the appearance, but judge righteous judgment." — John 7:24.

Everything you deal with in life has a reality world in which you live, and a man-made world that parallels it in mirror form.

You were trained backwards.

You don't understand the laws, you don't understand the difference between fiction and reality. In man's world fiction is form; in God's world substance is fact.

God created you in His image and likeness as fact, man created the Form.

Man created an application Form for the registration of your body as fact. This application Form applies to the State for a Birth Certificate that certifies a Birth Report. But God did not tell you to register your body to the kings of this world.

When the psalmist David took a census of the men, and numbered them when he was told not to do so by God, 70,000 Israelites were slain at the "hand of the Lord" for the crime of registering to the king. (I Chronicles 12:1-14).

The king does not deal with your body, he deals with the Form, your application Form.

The king invites you to register your body to him; a violation of God's law. By registering your body to the king, you volunteer your body into servitude to the kings of this world.

When parents register their child, they are pledging

their **legal title** to the child to the State; to the kings of this world. Even though the child may think he is free, there is a Security Instrument that transfers **the title to the "thing"** (*the child's body*) to the king. As far as the king of this world is concerned, that **Certificate of Title** (*the Birth Certificate*) is the only "thing" they see. It's more important to them than God's reality, the child.

If they hold the **Security Instrument** — the title to little Johnny or little Jane, they are the **holder-in-due-course** of the Title to the "thing" that you thought belonged to you (*your child*).

The state holds legal title to everything you think you own. They are playing in the **securities world** — the only world that they can see.

The term "owner" is not what you think it is. They told you that you were the owner of what think you own. An "owner" has equitable title to the "thing", not legal title. **Legal title** gives the holder total control over the "thing". **Equitable title** gives the holder only possession and use of the "thing" — possession and use of the reality, but not possession of the Security Instrument that represent the actual legal title to the "thing" — the property.

Who always wins in court? The holder of the "title" or the possessor of the "thing"? The holder of the "title"; the holder of control.

Every transaction has a creditor and a debtor. Scripture tells us that **the debtor is servant to the master.** The creditor can do no wrong. He has legal title to his property — the "thing" — so he can do no wrong. Your thinking is wrong; you're seeing things backward. If you are not the creditor you are not in control. You gave control away. You gave legal title to the "thing" away, to the State.

A bankrupt can not have legal title to any "thing" because he is bankrupt; a bankrupt — by definition — is a debtor to a creditor.

The United States was declared bankrupt in 1933. But the bankruptcy didn't start in 1933, it began in 1782 when Benjamin Franklin, under the authority of the Continental Congress, signed a six year mortgage agreement with the English Crown — the first Treaty of Peace after the Revolutionary War that ended the Revolutionary War.

This treaty acknowledged that the Continental Congress on twenty-one separate occasions, had borrowed 18 million livres of money from the Crown through the Crown's agent in Paris, the Rothchild Bank.

The Treaty of Peace that ended the Revolutionary War in 1782 was signed in Paris in 1783.

The six year mortgage was to come due on January 1, 1788 and Congress knew that they couldn't pay the debt. So Congress convened the Constitutional Convention to reorganize the government to give the Crown a pledge of Securities to underwrite the debt so the Crown wouldn't call the Continental Congress on the loan.

CONSTITUTION: a contract in international commerce; it is not a people thing.

CONSTITUTOR: a person who transfers his debts to someone else. A "person" is a corporation according to law. The corporate UNITED STATES that held the debt, transferred its debt to the States, that became parties to the Constitution of 1787.

Article IV of the Constitution says that all of the treaties in existence at the time of the instrument (1787) are in full force and effect, regarding especially the six year mortgage to the Crown against the UNITED STATES. By that Article the mortgage was transferred from the Congress of the UNITED STATES to the States of the Union, and the States agreed to accept its obligations when they ratified the Constitution for the United States of 1787; their pledge to pay off the mortgage to the British Crown.

The British Crown holds a mortgage on all the King's prior colonies in America, a **priority agreement** that it is the first creditor to get paid.

The Founding Fathers reorganized the government before the debt was due so they wouldn't have to tell the people what was going on.

As soon as the Constitution was ratified, George Washington — under emergency war powers — went to Congress and created the First National Bank of the United States — a private national bank. The purpose of this bank was to hold the assets — the securities of the United States — as the **pledged collateral** on the mortgage. The bank was a private third party that held the assets to pay off the loan to the English Crown under international law. The bank was the **Receiver** for the Crown.

THE RESULT

The creditors of the bankruptcy are in charge.

During the bankruptcy the creditors run the corporation called the UNITED STATES. All the real officials of the government today (*as was Benjamin Franklin in his time*) are Esquires, **agents of the En-**

glish Crown.

In America today, Esquires run the legislative, executive and judicial branches of government as one, One World branch. These Esquires represent the creditor — the Crown — during the bankruptcy of the United States. They are complying with the law. It's **us patriots** in America who are violating the law when we criticize our masters who are ruling under God.

IN BONDAGE SEVENTY YEARS

Under International Law, if a nation cannot pay its debts, its debts are forgiven every 70 years.

Seventy deals with 10 and 7. Seven is completion, which is sabbatical time for individuals. Individual debts should be cancelled every seventh year. But a nation's sabbatical time is ten times 70, or every 70 years.

The mortgage was renewed in 1789.

1879 +70 years = 1859.

We could have come out of the bankruptcy in 1859, but the nation renewed and enlarged the debt to pay for the beginning Civil War.

The Civil War began in 1859.

1859 + 70 years = 1929,

We could have come out of the bankruptcy in 1929, but the nation renewed and enlarged the debt when the farmers pledged their lands to the public in exchange for public aid, supposedly, to "save" farming.

Franklin Delano Roosevelt instituted The New Deal and Land Control under emergency war powers to regulate farming and overcome the Depression, and it's still that way today.

The Great Depression began in 1929.

1929 + 70 years = 1999 (when President Clinton

was being impeached).

We could have come out of the bankruptcy in 1999, but the nation renewed and enlarged the debt when it unknowingly chose to remain a military Democracy instead of reverting to a constitutional Republic.

The Clinton Impeachment dealt with Public Policy as to whether or not Americans wanted to renew the bankruptcy of the Democracy to the English Crown, or whether Americans wanted to come out of the Democracy and its national debt and restore the Republic with the national debt discharged.

Three periods of 70 years = 210 years in bankruptcy. 210 deals with numbers 21 and 10. Twenty-one in scripture is "the time of Jacob's Trouble." Jacob served 7 years for Laban, 7 years for Lea, and 7 years for Rachel. **Ten times 21 years is 210 years, the time Israel spent in captivity, in Egypt.**

America is the New Testament Israel.

American's have been enslaved for 210 years in modern Egypt (*Babylon*). We were due to come out January 1, 2000 but the people unknowingly elected to remain in the bankruptcy to the Crown and retain the military Democracy of the UNITED STATES, and proceed with the New World Order.

Since the Public elected to continue the bankruptcy, after 210 years in captivity, We the People have been given the right to separate ourselves from the Public and its debt and become **Private Freemen once again** — to come out of the bankrupt Democracy via **CPR** (the Commercial Process of Redemption).

This is what Redemption is all about. But only a Remnant will come out. If you are trying to save the

UNITED STATES, it's not going to happen, it's already fixed on its course. But you can come out of Babylon before it goes down as the Book of Revelation says it will, and come into the Republic, anew.

"Come out of her, my people, . . . that ye receive not of her plagues." — Revelation 18:4.

16
Administrative Law

The UCC is Administrative Law that bases the rules for all commercial transactions. When one files under the UCC there is no controversy hence no court can become involved. The artificially contrived system is impotent when faced with an unlimited liability sovereign (a chief ruler having supreme power).

One accesses Commercial law by the simple process of asserting one's solemn oath sworn true, correct, complete and not misleading, on one's unlimited commercial liability as a real flesh-and-blood, sentient being.

The first and critical step is to redeem the legal title (ownership) to your strawman. Your property identified as the all-capital-letter trade-name vessel created by the government on the day of your birth.

LEGAL FREEDOM

What you know can't hurt you because you can use your knowledge of the truth to "set yourself free" (John 8:32). But what you do NOT know can kill you. <u>Ignorance is potential suicide</u>. Do not consent to being enslaved if you do not want to be enslaved.

CONTRACT

All law is contract. Contract makes the law. To make a contract valid, the consent of the parties must be free, mutual, and communicated. Consent is not real or free when obtained through duress, menace, fraud, undue influence, or mistake.

The crucial and incurable flaw in all contracts is the absence of <u>full disclosure</u> and a true <u>meeting of the minds</u>, and <u>mutual good faith</u>. This absence constitutes fraud. Lenders do not disclose the fact that they do not loan out their funds. They do not operate in good faith. They are collection agents on contracts that are deceitfully devised and incomplete. There is usually no genuine agreement between the parties based on truth.

THE DECEIT

In order for a contract to be valid it must be entered into with <u>full disclosure</u>, <u>good faith</u> and <u>clean hands</u>.

However, the banks (and other lending institutions) lead you to think that you borrow their money and give them the right to your property should you default. What they willfully, intentionally and deceitfully do not disclose is the fact that member banks of the Federal Reserve are not allowed to make loans. They simply exchange your promise for another promise; no legal tender (cash) changes hands.

You promise to pay a sum of money to the bank over a period of time, plus interest, — you sign a promissory note and the bank credits your account with debt obligations — fiat money. YOU create the "money" when you sign the promissory note — the loan agreement; the credit card agreement, etc. — and give it to the bank, then they give the money YOU created by signing your note back to you, with interest and property claims attached. This is called "<u>The Bait & Switch</u>."

Your promissory note is posted on the banks books as a debt that you will have to repay. But this debt with its usury obligation and its claim against your property (your collateral) is obtained by the bank under false pretenses with no consideration (real money) involved. The bank converts <u>your signature</u> (your credit/asset) into a liability (a debt) that you will have to pay to them over time plus interest. If you fail to do so, the bank will take your property (your collateral) from you.

You allow the bank to take <u>your property</u> (your signature) and give it back to you in a changed form with strings attached. Your promissory note is evidence of the bank's claim against your future labor. Moreover, the bank can sell your promissory note up-front for cash. Then when they collect your payments they get paid a second time. And if you default, they will foreclose on your property and get paid a third time when they sell it at discount to someone else and claim you still owe the balance to them.

<u>You take all the risk</u>. For the bank to put your property at risk without full disclosure, good faith or clean hands is the equivalent of plunder, counterfeiting, and theft. The bank does not loan you their money; they sell your note and give your money back to you, expecting you to give it back to them in payments, plus interest.

The bank does not loan you <u>money</u>; it loans you YOUR <u>credit</u> instead of theirs.

REMEDY: Offer & Acceptance
<u>Offer</u>: 1. The act or instance of presenting something for acceptance. 2. A display of willingness to enter into a contract on specified terms, made in a way that would lead a reasonable person to under-

stand that an acceptance having been sought will result in a binding contract.

Acceptance: An agreement, either by express act or implication from conduct, to the terms of an offer so that a binding contract is formed. An unconditional acceptance = a contract.

If an acceptance modifies the terms or adds new terms, it operates as a counteroffer, not an acceptance. A conditional acceptance = a counteroffer.

When you send a check marked "final payment" on an account, you are making an offer for the bank to accept. The bank can respond in two ways.

1. If the bank cashes your negotiable instrument marked "final payment" it is accepting your offer (claim) that it is a final payment; the bank is agreeing with you on your terms.

2. If the bank refuses to accept your negotiable instrument marked "final payment" then your account is legally paid in full in accord with the UCC § 3-603. Either way you win.

UCC § 3-603 says that when a tender of payment to a person entitled to enforce the instrument is made, the effect of the tender is governed by the principles of law that apply to a simple contract. If the tendered payment is refused, there is discharge of liability for the payment debt. The debt is now transferred to the one who refuses to accept the instrument.

MAXIM: **A payment tendered and refused is paid in full.**

According to HJR-192 (House Joint Resolution 192), passed by Congress in 1933 and still in force today: It is public policy not to pay a debt. It is impossible to do so with real money. No person can compel anybody to pay a debt by tendering silver or gold. Once a debt is created it is never extinguished. Its obligation (its liability) is simply discharged: the debt is transferred from one party to the next by law.

With the advent of the bankruptcy and HJR-192 in 1933, it became no longer necessary or required to pay a debt. It is only necessary to discharge the liability set forth when it becomes due, by tendering another negotiable instrument by which the sum tendered (being sufficient in amount) discharges the liability of the underlying instrument.

OFFER AND ACCEPTANCE

MAXIM: **The Offeror is the tail and the Acceptor is the head.**

MAXIM: **You must go low to be made high.**

"For whosoever exalteth himself shall be abased; and he that humbleth himself shall be exalted." — Jesus at Luke 14:10,11.

MAXIM: **An offer refused is dishonored.**
MAXIM: **An offer commands a response.**

An Offer, being a presentment of something for acceptance, commands a response. And, there are three ways in which a person can respond.

He can (1) accept the offer as stated, (2) present a counteroffer, or (3) stand mute.

If he stands mute his silence is acceptance of the claim. A counteroffer must be of a higher priority than the offer.

NOVATION: 1. The act of substituting a new obligation for an existing obligation that replaces the existing obligation or of substituting a new party for an old party who replaces the existing party — (a substitute agreement). **2. The substitution of a new obligor for an existing obligor who has been discharged by the new obligee.**

It's called a **Novation** when you place yourself, a new obligor, in the position of your strawman, the previous obligor whose debt is now dischaged via the Commercial Process of Redemption (CPR).

No one can make a claim against you or your strawman after you both have been redeemed. Such a party would have **"failed to make a claim upon which relief can be granted."**

"Agree with thine adversary quickly, while thou art in the way with him; lest at any time the adversary deliver thee unto the judge, and the judge deliver thee unto officer, and thou be cast into prison. — Jesus at Matthew 5:25.

17
Public Bankruptcy

We are involved in a public bankruptcy, nationwide. This bankruptcy is being prosecuted in open court for all to see, yet few have figured it out.

On April 5, 1933 — by an Executive Order of the President — <u>in order to forestall a Second Civil War</u> — Congress passed House Joint Resolution 192. (HJR-192).

In every bankruptcy a receiver-trustee is appointed to represent the creditor's interests in the bankruptcy. This occurs without judicial intervention. It's called <u>re-organization</u> and occurs on a minute to minute basis whenever commerce is transacted — whenever a debt is transferred by assignment to someone else — whenever a charge of liability is *dis*-charged.

There is no money today. That which circulates on confidence alone is not money, it's just paper.

Redemptors are creditors, not debtors. Their UCC Contract Trust Account (CTA), when established, is <u>exempt from levy and prepaid</u> because the human industry that comes from our labor, our service, and our energy (our <u>credit</u>) is the only wealth that can discharge the debts of the society in which we live — the *Novus Order Seclorum* (the New World Order).

Our CTA is bonded and insured. Our <u>credit</u> facilitates the nation's commercial needs.

REGISTRATION

When you were registered with the corporate UNITED STATES you became a member of the public corporation by pledging (pawning) your energy and property to fund the economy and repay the federal debt.

You did not object to what others had pledged for you in your name without your knowledge and consent, because you have not known it.

This was the purpose of birth certificate registrations and other registrations. It registers you as the surety, or guarantor, for the obligations of your strawman. But now that you know this, you can redeem your Christian name via CPR — the Commercial Process of Redemption.

REDEMPTION

When you "file for record" your security agreement with your strawman on a UCC Financing Statement you become <u>a creditor of the bankruptcy</u> instead of being a debtor to the federal debt.

As a creditor, you can redeem yourself from the liabilities of the bankruptcy by accepting any draft, charge, or claim on the condition of "proof of claim."

When you become redeemed, a presenter cannot transfer his debt, duty or obligation to you without "proof of claim." He must <u>produce evidence that he has legal authority over you and your strawman</u>. This he cannot do because you hold the highest claim to your property and your strawman. You're the <u>holder-in-due-course</u> of your strawman and the results of everything he does and has ever done.

Fix these facts firmly in your mind:

<u>You are a creditor</u>. <u>A creditor never loses and a debtor never wins</u>. <u>A creditor has standing in law in the eyes of the State</u>. <u>A debtor does not</u>.

BANKRUPTCY

The First Rules of Bankruptcy:

Do not be an adversary or dishonor ensues. Dishonor converts the sovereign into the debtor who must pay or perform.

Do not create a controversy. Give honor where honor is due. OTHERS will forgive YOU only as YOU forgive THEM.

"Blessed are the peacemakers: for they shall be called the children of God" — Matthew. 5:9.

A CLASSIC EXAMPLE

When the IRS mails you a letter addressed to your strawman (your all capital letter trade-name), their intent is to entice you into their private domain via the way you acceptance their letter.

They want you to DISHONOR their draft by protesting it, thereby creating a controversy, or by ignoring it thereby agreeing to it as though it were true. Dishonor converts you from a sovereign into a debtor who must now pay or perform.

They want you to be the adversary — the debtor/looser — in the case.

As a creditor, you remain protected by the law — when you KNOW this, and claim it.

18
The Commercial Game

On April 5, 1933, then President Franklin Delano Roosevelt, under Executive Order, ordered:

"All persons are required to deliver ON OR BEFORE MAY 1, 1933 all GOLD COIN, GOLD BULLION and GOLD CERTIFICATES now owned by them to a Federal Reserve Bank, branch or agency, or to any member bank of the Federal Reserve System".

James A. Farley, Postmaster General at that time, required each Postmaster in the country to post a copy of the Executive Order (read Declaration) in a conspicuous place within each branch of the US Post Office. At the bottom of the posting was this warning:

"CRIMINAL PENALTIES FOR VIOLATION OF EXECUTIVE ORDER $10,000 fine or 10 years imprisonment, or both, as provided in Section 9 of the Order."

Section 9 of the Order read as follows:

"Whosoever willfully violates any provisions of this Executive Order or of these regulations or of any rule, regulation or license issued thereunder may be fined not more than $10,000, or if a natural person, may be imprisoned for not more than 10 years, or both; and any officer, director or agency of any corporation who knowingly participates in any such violation may be punished by a like fine, imprisonment, or both.

Stated within a written document received September 17, 1997 from the U.S. Department of Justice, Office of Legal Counsel, Office of the Deputy Assistant Attorney General, Richard L. Shiffin, in response to a FOIA, was the following:

> "A fact that is frequently overlooked is that Executive orders and proclamations of the President normally have no direct effect upon private persons or their property, and instead, normally constitute only directives or instructions to officers or employees of the Federal Government. The exception is those cases in which the President is expressly authorized or required by laws enacted by the Congress to issue an Executive order or proclamation dealing with the legal rights or obligations of members of the public. Such as issuance of Selective Service Regulations, establishment of boards to investigate certain labor disputes, and establishment of quotas or fees with respect to certain imports into this country."

It is obvious that President Roosevelt was not "expressly authorized or required" to issue an Executive order or proclamation demanding the public (private) to relinquish their privately held gold.

The order (dictatorial proclamation) issued by Roosevelt was an undisciplined act of treason.

On June 5, 1933, two months AFTER the Executive Order, the Senate and House of Representatives, 73d Congress, 1st Session, at 4:30 pm approved House Joint Resolution (HJR) 192: Joint Resolution

To Suspend The Gold Standard And Abrogate The Gold Clause, Joint Resolution to assure uniform value to the coins and currencies of the United States.

HJR-192 states, in part:

> "Every provision contained in or made with respect to any obligation which purports to give the obligee a right to require payment in gold or a particular kind of coin or currency, or in any amount of money of the United States measured thereby, is declared to be against public policy, and no such provision shall be contained in or made with respect to any obligation hereafter incurred. Every obligation, heretofore or hereafter incurred, whether or not any such provisions is contained therein or made with respect thereto, shall be discharged upon payment, dollar for dollar, in any such coin or currency which at the time of payment is legal tender for public and private debts."

HJR-192 goes on to state:

> "As used in this resolution, the term 'obligation' means an obligation payable in money of the United States; and the term 'coin or currency' means coin or currency of the United States, including Federal Reserve notes and <u>circulating notes</u> of Federal Reserve banks and national banking associations."

HJR-192 <u>superseded</u> public law (what passes as law today is only "color of law") replacing public law with public policy. This eliminated our ability to <u>pay</u> our debts, allowing only for their <u>discharge</u>. When we use any commercial paper (checks, drafts, warrants, federal reserve notes, etc.) and accept it as money, we simply pass the liability of the unpaid debt attached to the paper on to others by way of our purchases and transactions. This liabillity of the unpaid debt, under public policy, is the public liability for its collection. In other words, all debt is now public debt.

The United States government, in order to provide necessary goods and services, created a commercial bond (promissory note) by pledging the property, labor, life and body of its citizens, as payment for the debt (the bankruptcy). This commercial bond made chattel (government owned property) out of every man, woman, and child in the United States. We became nothing more than "human resources" and collateral for the federal debt. This was done without our knowledge and/or our consent. How? It was done through the filing (registering) of our birth records!

The United States government — actually the elected and appointed administrators of government — took (and still take to this day) certified copies of our birth records and place them in the United States Department of Commerce, as registered securities. These securities, each of which carries an estimated $1,000,000 value, have been (and still are) circulated around the world as collateral for loans, entries on the asset side of ledgers, etc., just like any other security.

There's just one problem — we didn't authorize it.

The United States is a District of Columbia corporation. In Volume 20: Corpus Juris Sec. 1785 we find "<u>The United States government is a foreign corporation with respect to a State</u>" (*NY re: Merriam 36 N.E.*

505 1441 S. 0.1973, 14 L. Ed. 287). Since a corporation is a fictitious "person" (it cannot speak, see, touch, smell, etc.) it cannot by itself function in the real world. It needs a conduit, a "transmitting utility," a liaison of some sort, to connect the fictitious "person" to the real world in which we live. Why is this important?

LIVING people exist in a real world, not a fictional virtual world. But government exists in a fictional world and can only deal with other fictional or virtual persons, agencies, states, etc. In order for a fictional "person" to deal with real people there must be a connection, a liaison, a *go-between.* This can be something as simple as a contract. When both "persons," the fictional and the real, agree to the terms of a contract, there is a *connection,* intercourse, dealings, there is *communication,* an exchange. There is *business.*

But there is another way for fictional government to deal with the real man and woman — through the use of a representative, a liaison, the go-between. Who is this go-between that connects fictional government to real men and women? It's a government created shadow, a fictional man or woman having the same names as ours.

This PERSON was created by using our birth certificates as the MCO (Manufacturer's Certificate of Origin) and the state in which we were born as the POE (Port of Entry). This gave fictional government a fictional PERSON with whom to deal directly.

This PERSON (vessel) is a STRAWMAN.

STRAMINEUS HOMO: Latin — A man of straw, one of no substance, put forward as bail or surety. This definition comes from Black's Law Dictionary,

6th Edition, page 1421. Following the definition of STRAMINEUS HOMO in Black's we find the next word, STRAWMAN.

STRAWMAN: A front, a third party who is put up in name only to take part in a transaction. Nominal party to a transaction, one who acts as an agent for another for the purpose of taking title to real property and executing whatever documents and instruments the principal may direct. The PERSON who purchases property for another to conceal the identity of the real purchaser or to accomplish some purpose otherwise not allowed.

Webster's Ninth New Collegiate Dictionary defines the term "STRAWMAN" as "a weak or imaginary opposition set up only to be easily confuted; or a person set up to serve as a cover for a usually questionable transaction".

The STRAWMAN can be summed up as an imaginary, passive stand-in for the real participant; a front; a blind; a person regarded as a nonentity. The STRAWMAN is a "shadow" go-between.

For quite some time a rather large number of people in this country have known that a man or woman's name, written in ALL CAPS, or last name first, does not identify real, living people. Taking this one step further, the rules of grammar for the English language have no provisions for the abbreviation of people's names, i.e. initials are not to be used. As an example, John Adam Smith is correct. ANYTHING else is not correct. Not Smith, John Adam or Smith, John A. or J. Smith or J.A. Smith or JOHN ADAM SMITH or SMITH, JOHN or any other variation. NOTHING but John Adam Smith identifies the real, living man.

All other appellations identify either a deceased man or a fictitious man such as a corporation or a STRAWMAN.

Over the years, government, through its "public" school system, has managed to pull the wool over our eyes and keep us ignorant of some very important facts. Because all facets of the media have an ever increasing influence in our lives, and because media is controlled (with the issuance of licenses, etc.) by government and its agencies, we have slowly and systematically been misled to believe that any form (appelation) of our name is, in fact, still us as long as the spelling is correct. This is not true.

We were never told (with full and open disclosure) what our government officials were planning to do, and why.

We were never told that government (<u>the corporate United States</u>) is a corporation, a fictitious "person".

We were never told that government had quietly, almost secretly, created a shadow STRAWMAN for each and every American, so that government could not only control the people, but also raise an almost unlimited amount of revenue — so it could continue, not just to exist, but to expand and GROW.

We were never told that when government deals with the STRAWMAN it is not dealing with real, living men and women.

We were never told (openly and clearly with full disclosure of all the facts) that since June 5, 1933, we have been unable to pay our debts.

We were never told that we had been pledged (and our children, and their children, and their children) as collateral, mere chattel, for the debt created by government officials who create treason in doing so.

We were never told that they quietly changed the rules, even the game itself, and that the world we perceive as real is in fact a fiction — and its all for the benefit of the government.

We were never told that the STRAWMAN — a fictional person, a creature of THE STATE — is subject to all the codes, statutes, rules, regulations, ordinances, etc. decreed by government, but that WE, the real man and woman, are not.

We were never told that we were being treated as property, as slaves (albeit comfortably for some) while living in the land of the free — and that we could easily walk away from the fraud.

We were never told we were being abused.

There's something else you should know: Everything, since June 1933, operates in COMMERCE. Why is this important?

Commerce is based on agreement, on contract.

Government has an implied agreement with your STRAWMAN (the government's creation) and your STRAWMAN is subject to government rule, as we illustrated above. But when we, the real flesh and blood man and woman, are enticed into their "process" we become the "surety" (co-signer) for the fictional STRAWMAN.

Reality and fiction are reversed. We then become liable for the debts, liabilities and obligations of the STRAWMAN, relinquishing our real, protected by the Constitution, character as we stand up and answer for our (their) fictional STRAWMAN.

So that we can once again leave our fictional STRAWMAN in the fictional world and replace ourselves in the real world, with all our "shields" in place against the fictional government, we must send a non-negotiable (private) "Charge Back" and a non-negotiable "Bill of Exchange" to the United States Secretary of the Treasury, along with a surrendered copy of our birth certificate, the evidence, the MCO of our STRAWMAN.

By doing this we discharge our portion of the public debt, releasing us, the real man or woman, from the debts, liabilities and obligations of the STRAWMAN. Those debts, liabilities and obligations exist in the fictional commercial world of "book entries" on computers and/or in paper ledgers. It is a world of "digits" and "notes," not of money and substance. The property of the real man becomes tax exempt and free from levy, in accord with HJR-192.

Sending the non-negotiable Charge Back and Bill of Exchange activates our UCC Contract Trust Account (CTA). What is our CTA? Let's go to Title 26 USC and take a look at section 163(h)(3)(B)(ii), $1,000,000 limitation:

*"The aggregate amount treated as **acquisition indebtedness** for any period shall not exceed $1,000,000 ($500,000 in the case of a married individual filing a separate return)."*

This $1,000,000 insurance account is for the STRAWMAN, the fictional "person" with the name in all caps and/or last name first. It is there for the purpose of making book entries, to move figures, "digits," from one side of ledgers to the other. Without constant movement a shark will die. Figures, digits, the entries in ledgers must move from asset side to debit side and back again, or commerce dies. No movement, no commerce.

The fictional persona of government can only function in a fictional commercial world, one where there is no real money, only **credit (fictional funds)** — mere entries, figures, digits.

Corporate (STATE) courts only have jurisdiction over the STRAWMAN. A presentment from fictional government — from traffic citation to criminal charges — is a *negative* commercial "claim" against the STRAWMAN. This "claim" takes place in the commercial fictional world of government. "Digits" move from one side of your STRAWMAN account to the other, or to a different account. This is today's commerce.

In the past we have addressed these "claims" by fighting them in court, with one "legal process" or another, and failed. We have played the futile, legalistic, dog and pony show — a very clever distraction — while the commerce game plays on.

But what if we refuse to play the dog and pony game, and play the commerce game instead? What if we learn how to control the flow and movement of entries, figures and digits for our own benefit? Is that possible? And if so, how? How can the real man in the real world function in the fictional commercial world in which the game exists?

When in commerce do as commerce does — use the Uniform Commercial Code (UCC). The UCC-1 Financing Statement is the one contract in the world that CANNOT be broken and it is the foundation of the Accepted for Value process. The power of this document is awesome.

Since the CTA exists for the STRAWMAN — who, until now, has been controlled by the government — WE can gain control (and ownership) of the STRAWMAN by filing a UCC-1 Financing Statement and activating the CTA. This does two things for us.

First, by activating the CTA we gain limited control over the digits in the account. This allows us to also move entries, figures and digits, for OUR benefit.

Secondly, by properly filing a UCC-1 Financing Statement we become the "holder in due course" of the STRAWMAN. A filed UCC-1 is public notice of a registered lien (by a real human being who becomes the secured party) upon the STRAWMAN who becomes a non-registered government created foreign corporation. With the STRAWMAN under our control, government has no access to the UCC CTA and they lose their go-between, their liaison, their connection to the real living man and woman.

From then on, when presented with a "claim" (a presentment), we can ACCEPT IT FOR VALUE (agree with it). This removes any judicable controversy. By doing this we remove the negative claim against our account and become the "holder in due course" (owner) of the presentment. As holder in due course you can require the sworn testimony of the presenter of the "claim" (under penalty of perjury) and request the account be properly adjusted.

You no longer have liability for your STRAWMAN. If you do commercial assignments, you have an asset (a Bill of Exchange) which you can spend. The birth certificate represents the fictional strawman. The SSN represents the commercial account. Behind every birth certificate is a $1,000,000 bond of pre-paid credit for any activity of your STRAWMAN.

When you employ your STRAWMAN and anyone else charges against HIM, that is a commercial trespass. If anyone goes after your STRAWMAN and wins any monetary award against the fiction (your STRAWMAN) then you (the real person secured party) get the first $1,000,000 of that charge since you have the priority first lien.

It's all business, a commercial undertaking, and the basic procedure is not complicated. In fact, it's fairly simple. We just have to remember a few things.

<u>This is not a "legal" procedure</u>; we're not playing the dog and pony show. <u>This is "commerce"</u>, and we're playing by the rules of the game. We accept the "claim," become the holder in due course, and challenge whether or not the presenter of the "claim" has the proper authority (the Order) to make the claim (to debit our UCC CTA account) in the first place. When they cannot produce the Order (they never can, an order was never issued) we request the account be properly adjusted (and the charge or claim goes away). Always Accept for Value, become the holder-in-due-course; do not prosecute yourself via your strawman.

If the presenter doesn't adjust the account, ask where the funds in question were assigned by requesting the Fiduciary Tax Estimate and the Fiduciary Tax Return for this claim. Since the claim has been accepted for value and is pre-paid and is exempt from levy, requesting the Fiduciary Tax Estimate and the Fiduciary Tax Return is in order because the information is necessary to determine who is delinquent and/

or making claims on the account. If there is no record of the Fiduciary Tax Estimate and the Fiduciary Tax Return, then request the individual tax estimates and individual tax returns to determine if there is delinquency.

If you receive no favorable response to your requests, you can file a *currency report* on the amount claimed/assessed against your UCC Contract Trust Account and begin the commercial process that will force them to either do what is required or lose everything they own.

This is the power of contracts in commerce.

A commercial contract overrides the Constitution, the Bill of Rights and any other document except a superior contract. No process of law — "color" of law under the present codes, statutes, rules, regulations, ordinances, etc. — can operate upon you. No agent or agency of government, including the courts, can gain jurisdiction over you **without your consent**. Don't give it. You are no longer in their fictional domain.

The Accepted for Value process gives you the ability to deal with "them," via your transmitting utility, go-between, STRAWMAN — and hold them accountable in their own commercial world for any action they attempt to take against you. Without a proper Order — (they don't possess such a document) — they must leave you alone or pay the consequences.

By knowing the difference between our real self and our STRAWMAN, and behaving accordingly, we redeem our rightfull sovereignty over "legal fictions" and the ability — which is our birthright — to prove and demonstrate our freedom.

19
The Private Domain

"Whosoever shall exalt himself shall be abased; and he that humbleth himself shall be exalted." — Jesus, at Matthew 23:12.

Just as there are two sides to every coin, there are two sides to the commercial venue — the private and the public domains.

In the public school system we were taught to function in the public domain. We were told nothing about the private domain — the private domain did not exist to us. A redemptor must learn how to function in the private domain, because Redemption is a state of mind.

In the world of commerce there are only debtors and creditors. Creditors are high; and debtors are low. Creditors have the commercial energy to act when they're charged; and debtors do not, — until they're charged as a creditor to act.

To energize a debtor, the creditor must transfer his commercial energy (his credit) to the debtor by going low as a debtor, to energize the debtor to become a creditor who can act.

The creditor must go low (humble himself) to make the debtor high with honor, transforming him into a creditor who then can act.

If the creditor doesn't go low (humble himself); and remains high as a creditor, there is no transfer of credit (the creditor's energy) to empower the debtor to do something for him. The debtor remains a debtor (dead) unable to act.

MAXIM: **You must go low to be made high.**

"Humble yourselves in the sight of the Lord, and he shall lift you up." — James, at James 4:10.

When the creditor goes low to make the debtor high, the debtor is energized with credit as a creditor who can then go low again as a debtor, honoring the creditor in return.

MAXIM: **Creditors never lose; debtors never win.**

It is therefore important to stay in control — to be the creditor in the end — to stay out of the public domain — to stay in the private domain of the commercial world.

In the commercial world we are dealing with Notes.

Notes are delivered to you to entice you to act as a creditor to energize their dead system by way of your "**sign of authority** (**credit**)" — your signature. They draft you to respond with a presentment.

To your strawman the presentment is a bill, but to you, a redemptor, it is an offer of credit you can accept or reject. If you accept the offer you bestow honor and remain in control, but if you reject the offer you dishonor the presenter and lose by default — due to your dishonor — and you become liable for the bill.

MAXIM: **You must give honor to get honor.**

"Honour all men. Love the brotherhood. Fear God. Honour the king." — Peter, at 1 Peter 2:17.

A **bond** is evidence of indebtedness.

Your UCC Declaration is a **bond** registered in the public domain, showing your private relationship to the public domain. Your UCC Declaration is an **indemnity bond** insuring you from commercial liability. If someone accuses you of something, your UCC filing is a **maritime insurance bond** that indemnifies you for the claims of your **vessel-strawman.**

INDEMNIFY: **To reimburse a person's loss from a third party's actions or defaults.**

My Insurance Declaration **indemnifies** (reimburses) a me for the losses I suffer because the State won't allow me to pay my strawman's debts (with silver or gold); I can only discharge them with **promissory notes**.

A strawman is a debtor whose redemptor becomes his creditor when his redemptor has been redeemed.

When a strawman commits a chargeable offense, his redemptor is indemnified by the state. What's more, **bonds that are registered are tax exempt.** A redenptor's bond creates a **tax exemption** for him.

When a strawman is charged, his account is out of balance; so to balance the account the charge must be discharged with an execution of law, to satisfy the claim. This discharge is an execution in the public domain that zeroes-out the account.

Your bond is an insurance policy — Public Policy HJR-192 of 1933.

Public Policy indemnifies (bonds) your liability by discharging your charges for you because it prohibits you from paying your debts. Your exemption comes from your bond in the public domain.

House Joint Resolution 192 is the **Public (Insurance) Policy of the United States** — the **consideration** for the government's draft to surrender the gold (and the gold statute). Therefore . . .

MAXIM: **He who has the gold pays the bills.**

The international bankers left us unable to pay our bills. If we can't pay them; we just can't pay them.

MAXIM: **No one can be compelled to do the impossible.**

Therefore, the international bankers must pay the debts that a redemptor can't pay. When the bankers took away our money (silver and gold) they made it impossible for us to pay our debts so they gave us with a <u>REMEDY IN LAW</u> — <u>Public Policy # HJR-192 Insurance</u> to discharge our debts, instead.

If you **lose something**, or you **can't use something**, or you **can't replace something** that's covered by insurance, **your insurance policy REDEEMS you from your loss.** So, when you can't pay your debts, **Insurance Policy HJR-192** discharges (forgives) your debts, instead. The international bankers took your money (silver and gold) away making it physically impossible for you to pay your debts, therefore **your Insurance Policy — HJR-192 —** forgives your inability to pay.

If someone charges your strawman with a debt, the first thing a redemptor should do is **accept the charge, acknowledge the charge, and return the charge discharged.** The tender is an unconditional offer of the presenter's credit to you to satisfy the charge the presenter created himself, by his signature.

A presentment is an offer put forward for acceptance.

The refusal of an offer dishonors the presenter and **puts the refuser in default** making him liable for the charge. **Accept the charge and return it to the presenter discharged via Public Policy HJR-192 by the international bankers who have the gold.**

Those who have the gold must pay the debts. Public policy is the **supercedeous bond** that discharges a redemptor's (a redeemed man's) debts.

MAXIM: **A contract = a bond, — a bond = a contract, — public policy = an unbeatable contract bond.**

A security agreement underlies your **UCC declaration**. The security agreement with your strawman is the basis of the security. You are registering the **security-bond-contract** in the public domain. When you register the **security-bond-contract** it becomes exempt from taxation.

Taxation is a debt that is exempt from payment by a redemptor. **Filing a UCC statement confirms the redemptor's exemption as a third party witness.** He is exempt because he is the **Secured Party Creditor (the principal)** registered in the commercial registry in the public domain. The redemptor is **"first in line and first in time"** to be paid. **The principal is not required to return interest to himself because the interest already belongs to him.**

Taxes are nothing more than the return of interest to the principal.

The registration of the **UCC statement** in the public registry makes the registered creditor the **"holder-in-due-course"** (owner) of the title to the goods or other items described in the security contract. **The principal has executed his rightful claim to be the principle holder of his estate.**

The Secretary of State is the registered agent of the Industrial Society and the UCC venue. The principal is the **settler** of his estate and the **sole beneficiary** of the public claim.

The public can claim you as a dependent (a debtor), **and utilize your exemption** (in your place), **simply by having your name on an unpaid account,** *unless you object.*

Redemption in Law is a state of mind.

Filing your **UCC statement** in the public domain is the best way to make it part of **the public record that has to be recognized** by every official in the public domain. **This statement is necessary for its perfection.**

Giving public officials **evidence** of your **non-negotiable, private-claim** is the only way to perfect that claim.

"Humble yourselves under the mighty hand of God, that he may exalt you in due time." — Peter, at 1 Peter 5:6.

20
Your Name Is Your Bond

Big Brother's Master Plan to subject the human race depends upon the people continuing to volunteer for, and finance, their own enslavement.

Without such voluntary giving from the public sector, our chosen masters face the exposure of their crimes. Heretofore, system operatives have been overwhelmingly successful at duping unwitting victims into volunteering for virtually every kind of financial exploitation imaginable. All on a voluntary basis.

In 1933 we converted from **substance backed currency** (gold) to **promise backed currency** (credit) to drive all players, except a favored elite, into bankruptcy, where only the fittest in the commercial game survive.

Everyone is competing for the same RATIONED amount of Federal Reserve Notes (FRN's), attempting to stay afloat in a sea of debt and avoid bankruptcy.

This is an intentional state of war in the game of life. The only way to stay in the game and avoid bankruptcy is to obtain more FRN's from the other players in the game — like a Monopoly game wherein but one party wins in the end (the elite).

All fiat money is borrowed into existence, and more money is owed than physically exists, because the principle amount is borrowed, but the interest due on it is not. Interest payments have to come from the principle borrowed, thus depleting the money supply, requiring additional borrowing in an never ending spiral into more and larger debt.

The most devastating form of volunteering occurs when you unknowingly promise to be responsible for and pay someone else's debt. This is how every unaware individual seals his fate. The **"trade-name-game"** involves an unthinking twin that works hand in hand with it. The legal masters of the world are aware of the distinction between your *true-name* and your *trade-name,* and have come up with an brilliant, ingenious device for exploiting the difference between these two names without tipping their hand.

The reason why the name on every driver's license, social security card, utility bill, etc., is set in all capital letters — converted from proper English into *legalese* — the reason why all banks insist on listing all accounts, not in the true-name of the party who walks in and fills out the forms, but in the ***artificial-trade-name*** associated therewith — is to conduct business with you via your unknown, invisible, corporately-colored, artificial-person strawman that is subject to all their statutory regulations, and therefore under their complete control — regardless of constitutional restraints.

The same applies equally when either of the two names are called out verbally. Differently constructed names comprise distinctly different items of property, however alike they may sound.

Most people believe that an "appellation" is nothing but an archaic synonym for a "name", e.g. "Christian appellation." The reason people have been generally led to misunderstand the meaning of this obscure term is the same reason that Big Brother calls himself a Sovereign and you his Subject, under political subjugation to compelled allegiance to the United States and the British Crown — when it is actually the other way around. You are the Sovereign, and Big Brother is Subject to you instead.

Most people have been taught to believe that whenever their name is called they are obliged to respond — as though the use of their name exerts ***unquestioning control*** over their lives. For example, calling the role in our public school taught us to unthinkingly respond to any mention of our name. A habit instilled in us with less than an innocent intent.

Your name is a piece of property. It can even be copyrighted so that no one else can use it without your permission and written consent. **You are not your "property". You are not your "name".**

An appellation is something that originates with someone else. **It is an offer for communication. It is a bid for control.** Others use your appellation to address you; to accost you; to get your attention. And how you respond to such an appeal for control is entirely up to you. **Your acknowledgment of your name surrenders jurisdiction and control to the jurisdiction of the one addressing you.**

People in America have lost sight of the fact that they are sovereigns, and that nothing can be foisted on them without their acknowledgement and consent (their agreement). This is a fact of life. **No one can legally victimize you without your consent.** People have lost sight of who the boss is and who the servant is, and who they really are.

Your name is a piece of property. It is not the living, breathing, flesh-and-blood man associated therewith. It is not you. When someone asks you for your name

— and you give it to him without thinking of the consequences — you voluntarily surrender your private property (your name) to the other party, and consensually and contractually pre-agree with whatever he wants to do with your name. If he is a judge in court, this can be dangerous. If you choose to respond when someone uses your name (your common-law-copyrighted-property) to get your attention, **you form an invisible contract with him without compensation, giving him jurisdiction over you** — and that is taken to mean your sovereign voluntary choice.

The world operates on the initiative of about 5% of the people (5 of each 100) and the remainder of the people need and want orders to perform. Such inert abstractions as governments, banks, tax agencies, courts, and corporations — all separate jurisdictional realms — have been accorded superiority over living beings by their voluntary consent. Governments are transitory mental contrivances set up by the clever few for the indirect purpose of, for the most part, living off the efforts of the trusting population.

The entire population of this country, and even this planet, has been systematically deceived through an inconceivably complex mechanism in the fields of commerce, law, and finance, by the same tribe of brilliant elite who are intent on your subjection and control. But you can now begin to deal with the situation as a self-governing fully accountable responsible woman or man who *can* control, and is *in control* of his or her own destiny, despite the odds stacked against the common man.

Knowing that **"You are not your name"** and that you, as sovereign, can take legal possession of your name in all its forms (like any other piece of private property) and that the option of accepting or rejecting any appellation from any party that comes your way is strictly yours in your sovereign capacity, will speed you on your course in life.

Your trade-name is your strawman, and you by default (as its surety) are responsible for knowing and complying with every letter of the law in every situation in existence because "Everyone is presumed to know the law", and "Ignorance of the law is no excuse."

If the **word-manipulators** who claim the legal title to the strawman with whom you are presumed to be contractually united, decide to tax, fine, regulate, rob, incarcerate and maybe even kill your strawman, then you, the living being, experience the consequences in reality. As surety for your strawman, you have no standing in law. A slave cannot sue his master or any other slave, because his master owns them both.

Men and women who are otherwise sovereign are unwittingly conditioned to **voluntarily contract** to be the surety for their strawman. Strawmen are severally and jointly responsible for the payment of the interest on the federal debt and the federal debt itself, making any man or woman with a social security number equally liable as co-surety for the payment of the federal debt, unless, of course, he or she objects.

The social security account is the strawman's account.

Social Security is neither an insurance contract nor a retirement program; it is a welfare program. Application for and use of a Social Security account number (SSN) is a tacit confession that one is incompetent to manage his or her own affairs; that he or she thereby appoints the U.S. government as his or her guardian and seeks eligibility for welfare payments.

Such status is known by other names as well, such as "child of the state" or "ward of the court," and is legally known as the doctrine of "parens patriae," where the state is considered to be the legal parent of those "under disability" and "unable to care for themselves." Your strawman — (and you by default as its surety) — is a child of the state, incapable of managing its own affairs and needful of guardianship — unless and until, that is, you repair the damage via the Commercial Process of Redemption (CPR).

Those who have paid social security taxes over their lifetime have no vested interest in social security. The payment of social security benefits is not obligatory — it is at the option of the state.

All of your commercial accounts are in the name of your strawman/trade-name. All of these accounts are your strawman's accounts. You are the accommodation party, the surety attached thereto. You are the party that everyone looks to for payment and performance, because you are the only one who can discharge your strawman's debts — unless you rectify the situation through the Commercial Process of Redemption (CPR).

The United States accepted custody of your name (your property) when you were born, and registered it via your original record of birth — your birth record. Your strawman was "berthed" (as a vessel) on the first document emitted by the government that referenced your name. Because everything about you is registered in the name of and accessed by your strawman/

trade-name, all your property is presumed to be your strawman's property as a public relations tool for maintaining order in the flock.

The entire planet functions in a mirror-image world of unreality, anchored by private notes that represent liability, not substance (i.e. Federal Reserve Notes; FRN's). We live in a private banking monopoly, on the non federal Federal Reserve. Government has no other way of doing business with us except via our strawman/trade-name.

Any presentment to you is either a demand for performance or acceptance — depending upon who you know you are.

In other words, a presentment is a demand for you to accept responsibility for paying or discharging someone's charge, or for the performance of some other act.

For instance, a police officer issues a charge against your strawman (a traffic ticket) demanding you to accept the responsibility of the officer's order to your strawman for him to appear and if necessary have you pay his ticket (discharge the charge). If at any point in the process you (the motorist) fail to accept responsibility for your strawman and the ultimate payment of the ticket (the charge against your strawman), then you (the motorist) are charged, arrested, and jailed in place of your strawman.

The acceptance of any presentment executes a contract between the offeror and offeree (the presenter and you). In the public sector, presentments are made by officials of the State. In the private sector, presentments are made by attorneys or other agents of the State for their employers.

Before anyone can issue a presentment to any strawman, the issuer of the charge must know the strawman's name. If the issuer cannot determine the name of a detainee, being held for questioning, within a brief period of time, he must release the detainee.

A sovereign's trade-name is the commercial entity under which he conducts business. His trade-name is his **private property** over which he has legal control. Any application he signs is a **voluntary gift of jurisdiction** to the public and the **establishment of a trade-name transaction account.**

When a government official says, "May I have your name?" he is asking you to give him the name of your **trade-name transaction account** so he can use it to make a charge against your **trade-name transaction account and you.**

Until redeemed, the flesh-and-blood man is surety for the party in whose name the **trade-name transaction-account** appears (his strawman) and he is held accountable for any charges incurred via his strawman's **trade-name transaction-account.**

The United States is bankrupt, and because of the fiat **money-by-decree** called Federal Reserve Notes (FRN's), commensurate changes in the realm of jurisprudence have taken place.

American tribunals are now **Federal Reserve Note tribunals** dealing exclusively in FRN's and enforcing the **private copyrighted corporate policy** of the owners of the FRN's, known as **public policy code.** All United States code is copyrighted British law copyrighted and owned by British corporations, some of which are located on American soil.

The American Revolution of 1776 was never ratified by referendum. Had it been put to a vote by the Founding Fathers, the rebels would have lost the decision to secede. Almost all of the Founding Fathers were esquires (attorneys) loyal to the British Crown.

The American Revolution was instigated and financed by their front-man financier, Caron de Beaumarchaise. (*National Geographic Magazine, July 1975, page 114*).

The international bankers bought themselves a country, they named the **UNITED STATES**..

UNITED STATES: 1) a name, 2) a (British) territory, 3) a collective term. — *Black's Law Dictionary, 6th edition.*

Now criminal as well as financial charges are commercial in nature. In Admiralty, the military enforces *criminal penalties* for *civil offenses.* The money-changers foreclosed on the federal United States in 1933, and use the **UNITED STATES** to prosecute their private, commercial interests for profit. We are under the military rule of the Commander-in-Chief of the military **"re-presented"** to us as the President of the United States.

Under Public Policy, which is military rule, we can be penalized VIA OUR STRAWMAN for any act even when no one is harmed and no property is damaged, e.g. for not wearing a seatbelt or for travelling 35 miles-an-hour in a 30 mile-an-hour speed zone.

Under common law, each man is in control of his own destiny as long as he does not harm another and thereby become obligated in some contract. Under common law each man is free to live as he sees fit, without interference from Uncle Sam (US).

Under Public Policy the police power is employed to penalize **behavior** (such as thought crimes) as well as **acts and deeds of substance**, for the purpose of extorting private "internal revenue".

When someone violates one's own sense of moral rightness, no matter how justified in the eyes of the law, one is dismembered by the police power of the State. Therefore, it behooves us to **re-assess** our lives and begin to rely on and use the power of the Commercial Process of Redemption (CPR) herein described.

This process is based on the power of common law, private property rights, and consensual contracts. This process has changed the course of every proceeding in which it has been introduced. Common law still exists in full force. It has simply been overlooked or intentionally mislaid.

21
Know Who You Are

In order to comprehend a thing, inquire first into its name, for a right knowledge of the thing depends upon its name.

> *"Good name in man or woman, dear my lord,*
> *Is the immediate jewel of the soul:*
> *Who steals my purse, steals trash;*
> *'tis something, nothing; 'Twas mine, 'tis his,*
> *and has been slave to thousands;*
> *But he that filches from me my good name*
> *Robs me of that which not enriches him,*
> *and makes me poor indeed."*

Othello, the Moor of Venice, Act III, Scene 3, by William Shakespeare.

JOHN J. DOE is not the same as John James Doe.

JOHN J. DOE is a fiction, and John James Doe is the name of the real man. John James is his given name and his family name is Doe.

Look at your driver's license and see to whom it really belongs. It is issued to your fictional strawman. Check your utility bill, it too is issued to your strawman, not to you.

The first name mentioned, JOHN J. DOE, is written in all-capital letters. It is a fictional front man acting in behalf of John James Doe. The real name, John James Doe, is written in cursive — caps and lowercase letters. The name, JOHN J. DOE, refers to a fiction and the real name, John James Doe, refers to the man.

"The first man is of the earth, earthy: the second man is of the Lord from Heaven. And as we have born the image of the earthy, we shall also bear the image of the heavenly." — 1st Corinthians 15:47,49.

"The last shall be first, and the first last ." — Matthew 20:16.

The Redemption of the soul includes protection from sin and the purification of righteousness attributed to the shed blood (sacrifice) of Christ. (I John 1:6,7).

"He is the faithful witness, and the first begotten of the dead, and the prince of the kings of the earth who loved us...and hath made us kings and priests unto God." — Rev. 1:5,6.

KNOW WHO YOU ARE

One's ability to perceive — one's awareness — is directly proportional to one's ethics. Humble though their station may be, some individuals observe what others do not; they look beyond the curtain of tyranny hiding human law and make sense of it — and convey their discoveries to others; perceiving what none had perceived before.

Laws today are called codes because they have been encoded from their original form so that the man on the street will be confused and not understand how to conduct himself and his affairs according to law.

Law is no longer law, but a cornucopia of code. The Uniform Commercial Code (the UCC) is the achievement of an uncountable number of dedicated collaborators over thousands of years. The UCC is the culmination of a far-reaching, global PLAN to obtain absolute, legal, financial, social, political, and ecclesiastical control over the peoples of the world — through the commercial domain.

"And he causeth all, both small and great, rich and poor, free and bond, to receive a mark in their right hand, or in their foreheads: And that no man might buy and sell, save he that had the mark, or the name of the beast, or the number of his name." — Revelation 13:16,17

Even so, there's no mechanism in the UCC that can ever bring about the recapture of we former slaves who managed to break free.

Redemption is deliverance from the power of an alien domination and the enjoyment of its resultant freedom. It includes the idea of being restored to the status of one who possesses a more fundamental right or interest. It is salvation from a state or circumstance that would impair or destroy the value of human existence or human existence itself.

The word "redeemer" and its related terms "redeem" and "redemption" appear in Scripture some 130 times. Although used to describe divine activity, these words arise in human affairs as well, and it is in this context that they must be first understood.

These words, as belonging to the domain of commercial law, refer to the exchange of an equivalent for what is secured or released. The relation of the agent to the object of redemption is always — in Scripture — a person or another living thing. Its usage in cultic activity does not differ from that of a normal commercial transaction. In both cases a person or an animal is released in return for money or an acceptable substitute.

The Christ Idea displaces the notion of lack, limitation, want and woe, sin, sickness, and death.

A CULTURAL OBSCURITY

Incredibly — even though it permeates and dominates the lives and everyday activities of every man, woman, and child in America, and virtually every living being on planet earth — and even though it's the most senior form of law in every country in the world — the UCC has been so brilliantly orchestrated by the legal masters of the world that it's become a cultural obscurity so well absorbed into society as to not even raise an eyebrow of interest upon its mention.

Even the general members of the Bar are for the most part ignorant of its far-reaching applications and implications that dominate their lives as well. Most likely you never even heard of the UCC until it was herein brought to mind.

By studying the UCC, it is possible for you to begin to gain control of your life and better protect your family, your property, and yourself.

Know then who you are.

22
Redemption in Law

"Karate for defense only." — Miagi [from the motion picture "The Karate Kid"]

You have been and now are the unknowing victim of an ingenious though ancient diabolical conspiracy of untold ramifications.

Americans have been and now are under the rule of undeclared martial law, since Abraham Lincoln declared martial law in 1861 and took over Congress and the government as Commander-in-Chief of the Armed Forces of the United States. Unbeknownst to you, all property ownership is in the hands of the state — the corporate United States (the federal zone) — Washington, D.C.

You do NOT own the property that you think you own — not your home, not your vehicle, not even your children! The state can take away your children and its other property (chattel) if you do not conform to the dictates and whims of the state and behave as the state sees fit — regardless of the Constitution, the Bill of Rights, and the common law.

All property in America belongs to the state just as the plank in the Communist Manifesto regarding property ownership declares. Right here in America the state has "legal title" to all your property while you have only an "equitable interest" in what you think you own — and that only on your good behavior.

As long as you give tribute (tax money) to the conquering state (as they demand) they will leave you alone to "enjoy" life, liberty and a so-called "pursuit of happiness" — but within the confines of the king's plantation — the public domain.

As a slave on the king's plantation, you work for him only — via the Company Store — the non federal Federal Reserve.

As a slave on the king's plantation you are subject to your master's legal but unconstitutional demands.

MAXIM: **The created is subject to the creator.**
MAXIM: **The borrower is subject to the lender.**
MAXIM: **The slave is subject to the master.**
MAXIM: **The debtor is subject to the creditor.**

The state has created your strawman for its own benefit and presumes that you have unknowingly contracted to be the surety (co-signer) for it (your state created fictional strawman). The state deals with your strawman and you go along for the ride. If your strawman is fined, you have to pay the bill. All your bills come to your strawman written in its all-capital lettered "war/trade-name." A name that sounds exactly like your name when spoken — your nom de guere "war-victim/trade-name."

JOHN Q. DOE does not mean the same in law as John Quincy Doe.

All commerce is conducted between the state and your strawman, and you are financially responsible for what your strawman contracts to do and does with or without your consent. Neat, isn't it, for the state? Your "strawman/government-slave" works not for you, but for the state. He (meaning you) has no "standing-in-law" because he is a slave and his master is the state.

You are his surety and the spokesman for what he does — with or without your consent. You are unknowingly **a ward of the state**.

No one can interfere with the contracts that we make whether constitutional or not.

The Constitution has little or no bearing upon commercial law even though it is based on commercial law. We can contract to do whatever we wish to do, and we have unknowingly contracted to be **a ward of the state**. But we can can **rescind** that silent contract and **redeem** our enslaved strawman from government control so that he will work for us, and no longer for the state.

Like an item pawned to the owner of a pawn shop, your strawman is waiting there to be redeemed by you. When you recapture your strawman you regain commercial control of your life. You are now a prince of the king, no longer his slave, — but you must first be aware that this plot against you really does exist.

Fictional entities can only deal with fictions. The court is a fiction and so is your strawman. The court cannot deal directly with you — only with an attorney "re-presenting" your strawman. When you have redeemed your strawman your status is reversed. YOU become your strawman's employer and the state becomes his surety instead and responsible for your strawman's debts and what he does. You, not the state, are your strawman's beneficiary now. You benefit from what your strawman does; not the state. Public presentments to your strawman are now bills to the state and receivables to you. The struggles, confusion, and grievances are no more. The courts can no longer control you when you tell the court who you are, a real flesh and blood, living woman or man. You are no longer under the state's control.

"Redemption-in-Law" is a "state of mind." It is a redemption of your commercial status with the state.

The moment you realize that you are a living, breathing, child of God under commercial law — and not your government created strawman — you and your strawman are then and there redeemed. You only have to make your new status known in the public domain.

You make public notice of this change in your status by transferring your strawman's birth-certificate-registration from the **corporate public domain** to the **incorporate private domain**. In other words, from the *martial-rule democracy* under which you now live to the *common-law republic* of the private side of life. Re-register your strawman's birth-certificate from the **public corporate side**, to the **private incorporate side** — via a UCC Declaration according to the universal Uniform Commercial Code (UCC).

Learn to live as a prince of the king, instead of as his slave.

You have just been introduced to the newly discovered revolution called "Redemption-in-Law."

Democracy can be changed back to the Republic for which our three-color flag-of-peace stands — our red, white and blue flag-of-peace — not the state's gold fringed military flag-of-war.

23
Who Am I?

Who am I? Am I of the Adam-dream? or am I of Christ who said, **"Before Abraham was I AM"?**

"That which I see not teach thou me: if I have done iniquity, I will do no more. Should it be according to thy mind? he will recompense it, whether thou refuse, or whether thou choose; and not I: therefore speak what thou knowest. Let men of understanding tell me, and let a wise man hearken unto me." — Job 34:32-34.

"One thing have I desired of the Lord, that will I seek after; that I may dwell in the house of the Lord all the days of my life, to behold the beauty of the Lord, and to enquire in his temple. For in the time of trouble he shall hide me in his pavilion: in the secret of his tabernacle shall he hide me; he shall set me up upon a rock. And now shall mine head be lifted up above mine enemies round about me; therefore will I offer in his tabernacle sacrifices of joy; I will sing, yea, I will sing praises unto the Lord. - Psalm 27:4-6.

"The thing that hath been, it is that which shall be; and that which is done is that which shall be done: and there is no new thing under the sun." — Ecclesiastes 1:9.

"For the multitude of dreams and many words there are also divers vanities; but fear thou God. If thou seest the oppression of the poor, and violent perverting of judgment and justice in a province, marvel not at the matter: for he that is higher than the highest regardeth; and there be higher than they." — Ecclesiastes 5:4,5,7,8.

"But by the grace of God I am what I am; and his grace which was bestowed on me was not in vain; but I laboured more abundantly than they all: yet not I, but the grace of God which was with me. Now if Christ be preached that he rose from the dead, how say some among you that there is no resurrection of the dead? But if there be no resurrection of the dead, then is Christ be not risen: And if Christ be not risen, then is our preaching vain, and your faith is also vain. Yea, and we are found false witnesses of God; For as in Adam all die, even so in Christ shall all be made alive." — 1 Corinthians 15:10,12-15,22.

"I therefore, the prisoner of the Lord, beseech you that ye walk worthy of the vocation wherewith ye are called, With all lowliness and meekness, with longsuffering, forbearing one another in love; Endeavoring to keep the unity of the Spirit in the bond of peace." — Ephesians 4:1-3.

"Wherefore, gird up the loins of your mind, be sober, and hope to the end for the grace that is to be brought unto you at the revelation of Jesus Christ ; As obedient children, not fashioning yourselves according to the former lusts in your ignorance. Because it is written, Be ye holy; for I am holy." — 1 Peter 1:13,14,16.

"I am the Alpha and Omega, the beginning and the end, the first and the last. Blessed are they that do his commandments, that they may have right to the tree of life, and may enter in through the gates into the city. I Jesus have sent mine angel to testify unto you these things in the churches. I am the root and the offspring of David, and the bright and morning star He which testifieth these things saith, Surely I come quickly. Amen." — Rev. 22:13,14,16, 20.

SINCE THE EARLY 1960s, state governments — created legal fictions signified by full caps — have issued birth certificates to "persons" with legal fiction, full caps names. This is not a lawful record of your physical birth, but of a legal fiction as signified by the use of the full caps name. It may look as if its a proper name, but that's not possible since no proper name is ever written in full caps. Your birth certificate is the government's created legal instrument indicating the government's legal title of ownership (or deed) to the legal fictitious "person" it has created just for you.

When you were born, the hospital sent the original (not a copy) of your birth record (record of live birth) to the state Bureau of Vital Statistics, sometimes called the Department of Health and Human Services (DHHS) of your state. Each STATE is required to supply the bankrupt UNITED STATES INC. with birth, death, and health statistics. The STATE agency that received your original birth record kept it and issued a birth certificate in the name of your government devised (not created by God) fictional alter ego (strawman "person") as signified by the full caps name (i.e., JAMES SMITH, not James Smith).

CERTIFICATE: "A document evidencing ownership or debt." — *Merriam Webster Dictionary 1998.*

Then your state issued birth certificate is registered with the U.S. Department of Commerce (part of the Executive Office) specifically through their own sub-agency, the U.S. Census Bureau that is responsible for registering vital statistics from all the states. The word registered as it is used within commercial or legal based equity law, does not just mean that the full caps name was merely noted in a book for reference purposes. When your birth certificate was registered with the U.S. Department of Commerce you became, at the same time, the surety or guarantor of the legal "person" (your straw man) named on it in full caps.

REGISTER: "An official record or list, such as a corporation's list of the names and addresses of its shareholders. — Also termed registry." — *Black's Law Dictionary, seventh edition.*

SECURITY: "Something given, provided, or pledged to make certain the fulfillment of an obligation; an evidence of debt or of property."— *Merriam Webster Dictionary 1998.*

SURETY: "A person who is directly liable for the payment of another's debt or the performance of another's obligations." — *Black's Law Dictionary.* "Under the Uniform Commercial Code a surety includes a guarantor, and the two terms are generally interchangeable." — *Merriam Webster's Dictionary of Law 1996.*

GUARANTOR: "One who makes a guarantee or gives security for a debt."— *Black's Law Dictionary, seventh edition.*

BOND: "A written promise to pay money or do some act if certain circumstances occur or a certain time elapses; a promise that is defeasible upon a condition subsequent." — *Black's Law Dictionary, seventh edition.*

In light of all this, it is not difficult to see that a state created birth certificate, written with full caps in the name of a "legal person" is a document evidencing debt the moment it is issued.

Once each state has registered your birth certificate with the U.S. Department of Commerce, the U.S. Department of the Treasury then issues Treasury Securities in the form of Treasury Bonds, Notes, and Bills using your birth certificate as surety or guarantor for these purported Securities. This means that the bankrupt corporate United States pledges, to the purchasers of its securities, the lifetime talents, labor, and property of all Americans as collateral for payment of the government's (not our) federal debt. They do this by converting your **lawful name** into a **legal person** — your strawman.

You are legally considered to be a slave or indentured servant to the various federal, state and local governments via your STATE issued and created Birth Certificate in the name of your full caps "person" (your strawman).

Your birth certificate was issued so that the state can hold exclusive title to your legal person (your strawman) from birth. This is compounded further when you "voluntarily" obtain a driver's license or a Social Security Identification number (SSN). They even own your personal and private life through your STATE issued marriage certificate issued in the names of "legal persons" (legal strawmen). You have no Rights (no standing) in birth, marriage, or even death. The government's creditors (the private owners of the non-federal Federal Reserve) hold the sovereign rights to all the fictional titles that the US Government has devised.

We have unknowingly but "voluntarily" agreed to their system (scheme) of legal fiction law by remaining silent and not claiming our Rights (a legal default). The rules and codes enforce themselves. There is no court hearing to determine if those rules are correct. Their "law" is self-regulating and self-supporting. Once set into motion, their laws automatically come into effect when the legal process has been followed.

The only asset the UNITED STATES INC. has in order to pay the federal (national) debt — their bankruptcy debt since even before to 1933 — is the people themselves. But if the UNITED STATES admitted this publicly, the people would never allow their labors and future to be collateral to this government created debt.

Instead, the US Government secretly pledged the future labor, property and tax revenues of the American people instead, by and through the full caps legal fictional "persons" they devised as collateral for credit — government borrowings from the non-federal Federal Reserve — to pay for its daily operational expenses and the interest (but never principle) on its ever increasing never ending, national (federal) debt.

"Waivers of constitutional rights must be voluntary, and knowingly intelligent acts, done with sufficient awareness of the relevant circumstances and likely consequences." — Brady v. United States.

ALL RIGHTS RESERVED

I will not be held accountable for any agreement that I did not willingly and voluntarily enter upon full disclosure of the facts.

24
Working With Drafts

Maxim: "**You must go low to be made high.**"

In commercial terms, to **"go low"** means to proceed as a debtor, and to **"go high"** means to proceed as a creditor.

The goal in commerce is to be the creditor holding the title to the *"res"* (*object*) of the transaction; to be in control.

The creditor of the *"res"* (*object*) of the transaction always wins if he follows the procedural rules.

A debtor has no **title** in the substantial world. He might have an **equitable privilege** (by contract) to use or possess the thing (property) for good behavior, but in any dispute over title in a commercial transaction, the debtor never wins.

The *debtor's* best day in court is to **postpone** the execution of judgment or collection of the debt or order to perform, to a future day. The *creditor's* best day in court is when the judgment is **not postponed** but is in his favor, so he can collect on it or force his opponent to perform.

A debtor cannot "win" because he has no commercial energy to act. The creditor has legal title to the substance of the transaction so he cannot lose. To be the creditor in the matter of title is the sovereign's goal.

How does one get to be a creditor of the legal title?

Legal Title to the *"res"* (*the property*) comes to one

by sale, inheritance, or some other method recognized in law. The issue is not how to *get* legal title, but how to *keep* it by the proper procedure after it is obtained.

Most people believe that you have legal title if you simply claim to be the title holder, or creditor, — that you acquire the status of creditorship by good intentions and words. But this is not procedurally true.

You become a creditor, not by words and good intentions, but by the actions and testimony of others who treat you as a creditor indeed.

So what is the procedure by which we gain creditor status? By the proper use of commercial drafts.

All interactions between people are commercial transactions that are governed by maxims of law. All transactions between people are commercial drafts.

A draft is like *an order; a command; a direction; an instruction; a request.* And there are three parties to a draft. A *drawer,* a *drawee,* and a *beneficiary.*

Most drafts are in *written* form but they can be *verbal* as well. In the public domain, a draft must be in written form and show intent unless spoken before witnesses.

The *drawer* is the debtor; the *drawee* is the creditor (the public or private banker); and the *beneficiary* is the party who benefits when the draft is fulfilled.

EXAMPLE ONE: THE BANK CHECK

All checks are drafts, but not all drafts are checks.

The **drawer** of the draft is the one who writes and signs the check; he is a debtor in the procedure to be carried out. The **beneficiary** is the one who will benefit from the funds when the check is cashed; the one to whom the check is written.

The **drawee** (the bank) is the one to whom the order is given to process the draft and cash the beneficiary's check; he is the creditor who has been drafted (energized) to act.

The drawer who drafts the check (or the traffic ticket, or the summons, or the claim) is the debtor in the procedure because he owes the beneficiary the money indicated by the draft. Although a debtor in the procedure the drawer is a creditor in substance regarding the funds upon which the check is drawn.

There is another reason why the drawer is a debtor in the procedure.

The bank's deposits are **public depositary** accounts, not **private repository** accounts.

When you deposit your funds in a bank you **lay down** (surrender) **legal title** to the funds and retain only **equitable interest** in the account. The bank accepts legal title to the funds that you laid down and becomes the creditor in the procedure. You are the debtor in the procedure because the funds that you laid down (deposited) are instruments of debt.

Debt instruments represent **debts**.

Warehouse receipts represent **assets.**

EXAMPLE TWO - COURT ACTIONS

All court actions are drafts. The plaintiff draws up a complaint (a draft) and presents it to the clerk for filing. The complaint is **an order to the court** that orders the court to confirm, or witness to, the complaint against the accused who has allegedly done something to justify the plaintiff's claim for relief.

All pleadings are commercial drafts.

The ***drawer*** of the draft is the one complaining to the court (the plaintiff). He is the ***beneficiary*** of the draft; the one who will benefit if a court order is drafted against the accused. The beneficiary is the pleader himself.

The ***drawee*** of the draft is the clerk of court because the clerk of court is made the "holder-in-due-course" of the draft. This makes the ***drawer*** (the pleader) a debtor and the ***drawee*** (the clerk) a creditor who can act, in this procedure of the case.

The ***pleader*** (the plaintiff) has laid down (surrendered) to the court his ***alleged title*** to the property he claims (if indeed and in fact he has legal title to the claim) to empower the court with jurisdiction over the judgment he seeks against the **accused** named as the defendant in the case, for a remedy.

Maxim: **The *offeror* of a contract is the *debtor* and the *acceptor* of the contract is the *creditor*.**

In all arguments (disagreements) the **creditor** has the **commercial energy** to throw the ball — and a public duty to perform. The debtor has no commercial energy so he remains at rest.

To play the game correctly you need to get rid of the ball (the charge) as soon as it is thrown to you.

As in the game of "hot-potato," return the ball (the obligation to perform) back to your opponent. When he drafts you with the ball, redraft it back to him.

When you are thrown the ball, you become the creditor who is charged (energized to perform). Your opponent makes you the ***drawee*** of the draft by going low thus making you high; he gives you honor; he honors you to repond.

Redraft the ball back to him by going low thus making him high; honoring him in return; making him the creditor who must act or be judged in default.

If the creditor fails to get rid of the ball, the referee of the game (the judge) will penalize him for "holding the ball" too long and obstructing (dishonoring) the game.

Dishonor converts a creditor into a debtor in defeat.

Get rid of the ball quickly. Do not keep it too long or you'll be penalized with default. If you dishonor your opponent the game ends and you lose. So...

"Agree with your adversary quickly." - Matthew 5:25.

When the clerk accepts the complaint from the plaintiff (the **drawer** of the draft), the clerk becomes the creditor of the draft and the "holder-in-due-course" of the draft; the ball is in her court so she has to get rid of the ball.

The clerk draws up a **summons** (a **second** draft) which she sends, with a copy of the complaint, to the accused. The commercial energy (*the charge*) that enabled the clerk to send the second draft to the accused, came from the **first** draft (the **original** charge) which was tendered to her by the plaintiff.

The **drawer** of the **second** draft two is the clerk of court, and the **drawee** is the accused. The clerk is now the debtor **and the accused is the creditor who is in control of the case.** Surprise!

Since the accused has the ball, he is now the creditor who is in control who must get rid of the ball or he will dishonor the court. But what does the accused do with ball instead? **he convicts himself.**

How does the accused convict himself? He holds the ball; *the obligation and energy to act,* and stands mute, or he argues the case. **He fails to** (1) **accept responsibility for the claim and he fails to** (2) **order** (redraft) **the court to release the plaintiff's order to the court** (the complaint that he now controls) **to him.**

By failing to redraft the court (by not returning the ball) **he convicts himself.**

The interesting thing about drafts is that to be honorable the drawee must ALWAYS accept the presentment (the complaint; the summons; the draft).

To *not* accept the draft is to dishonor its maker (its drawer) by creating a ***controversy*** (a ***dispute***). Disputes have to be settled to achieve peace — either ***peacefully*** (between the parties), or ***forcefully*** (by the court).

Consider the example of the check :

When a check is written on a bank the party who holds the check takes it to the bank for cashing or deposit. The bank, upon whom the check is written, will ALWAYS accept the check even if the check is no good.

The bank will ALWAYS accept the check from its presenter; this is called **"acceptance."**

The bank will stamp their mark on the check and search their records to see if the check is good — to see if the account exists and if there are sufficient funds in the account to cover the check and to be sure the account is not blocked. If there is no problem with the account and the presenter is properly identified then the bank will process the check which is a draft.

If there is a problem the bank will **"state a claim"** by redrafting the one who tendered the check to the bank for prodessing, with a redraft; (a counterclaim). Such a counterclaim might say, **"insufficient funds."**

This redraft is a **legal** (honorable) **reason** for the bank's failure to carry out the order of the draft, it is not a dishonor to the presenter. The counterclaim puts the ball back into the presenter's court.

By the redraft the bank becomes the **debtor** (honorably) and the presenter is again the **"holder-in-due-course"** of the check (the draft) to do with it as he wills. Had the bank accepted the check but failed to cash the check and failed to redraft the presenter with a legal (honorable) reason why the bank had not **cashed** (**honored**) the check, then the bank would move from being a party of honor to being a party of dishonor for the bank's **"failure to file a return"**..

Dishonor is a term of legal status, or condition, in the commercial venue. It occurs when the creditor in a commercial transaction, who has a duty to respond, does not respond within a given time limit, and therefore moves from a condition of honor to dishonor.

All court transactions are commercial transactions.

All crimes are commercial crimes, even murder and assault.

The party who expects action by the creditor on the order is a debtor in the transaction. The debtor is legally helpless as long as he remains the debtor and cannot act on the matter. However, **the law always provides a remedy.**

When the creditor who has a duty to act does not act in a given amount of time his dishonor creates a reversal in the commercial relationship between the parties of the case. **The roles are reversed.** The creditor becomes the debtor and the debtor becomes the creditor. This enables the drafting party (the drawer of the draft) to act to recover the commercial energy needed to seek a remedy for the dishonor.

Evidence supporting the reversal of relationships resulting from the dishonored draft is known as a **Notarial Protest** — an instrument in writing by a notary who as a third party testifies to the evidence of a dishonor as told to him by the holder-in-due-course of the dishonored draft.

Without evidence — without the **Notarial Protest** — there is no documented proof of the reversal of the commercial relationship between the parties in the dishonored draft. The lack of a **Notarial Protest** in the public record prevents (stops) the dishonored party from moving forward, and none of his subsequent motions (drafts) will be recognized until a proper **Notarial Protest** appears.

The dishonored party — the drawer of the dishonored draft — is a debtor with no commercial energy to pursue a remedy. The appearance in the record of the properly drawn **Notarial Protest** is the evidence that gives the dishonored party the commercial energy as a creditor to proceed with a new round of drafts to prove his counterclaim. If the accused does not submit a **Notarial Protest**, the judge will find him in default, therefore the accused convicts himself and the case is closed.

In the example above, if the accused — upon receiving the *summons* (the *second draft*) from the clerk — does not respond to the court within an appropriate period of time, then he dishonors the court, and the judge will enter a **Notarial Protest** of the accused's default because of his **"failure to file a return"** in answer to the complaint.

If the accused's answer contains an **"acceptance"** of the *summons* (the *second draft*) and a redraft to the court, his honorable answer throws the ball (the duty to perform) back to the plaintiff requiring him to **"prove his claim with evidence"** or stand mute. This throws the ball back to the court and releases the accused when the plaintiff defaults by **"failing to state a claim upon which relief can be granted."**

Courts today are not **constitutional courts** practicing common law. They are **commercial courts** practicing contract law under private international law.

Contrary to public teaching among patriots today, in the **Commercial Process of Redemption (CPR)** **"acceptance-for-value"** without a proper redraft is a **disaster** waiting to happen.

When you **"accept-for-value"** and request that "the order of the court be released to you," or when you **"accept-for-value on condition of proof of claim"** you are redrafting, and reversing their status.

Your request that "the order of the court be released to you" or your **"acceptance-for-value on condition of proof of claim"** is the required redraft. The **redraft** is as important as the **acceptance**.

If you accept without a redraft you remain the creditor holding the ball who has a duty to perform, and you'll be found in dishonor for **"failing to file a return"** in response to the second draft; regarding the claim presented to your strawman — or to you if you have not been redeemed.

25
A Knight's Tale

"We will... We will... rock you!
— We will... We will... rock you!"

IN MEDIEVAL TIMES a sport arose that was embraced by noble and peasant fans — though only noble knights could compete.

The sport was jousting.

For one of those knights, an over-the-hill former champion, it was the end, — but for his peasant squire, William, a thatcher's son, it was just the beginning.

As a young peasant lad, William saw his first knight's jousting tournament and tells his dad that he wants to be a knight when he grows up. An older peasant derides him and says: *"You will never compete in a tournament, you have to be a knight of royal blood to compete."* But the boy's father says to the lad, *"Don't pay any attention to him — you can change your stars — if he believes enough a man can do anything. You can change your stars."*

The stars the dad was referring to are "the descendants of Abraham." They (the stars) are subject to the laws of God and not to the laws of man.

Maxim: **Anything is possible; you can be what you want to be.**

To provide an opportunity for the young lad to reach his dreams, the father recognized that the young boy would have to leave home (his comfort zone) in order to get the training and experience he would need to become the knight that he desired to be. So the father arranged with an older knight to allow his son to be his page boy and serve him. The lad was seven (a number representing completeness).

Maxim: **You must go low to be made high.**

The father took his son to France, met the knight, and the following procedure transpired in a scene in the movie.

The father walks with his son from the small boat toward the old knight. The father introduces himself to the knight. The knight says: ***"Is this the boy?"*** This is a commercial draft. The knight is a debtor in the procedure. He is the drawer of the draft. The father is honored by being made the creditor.

The father, being the creditor with the responsibility to respond, responds. He says: ***"Yes"*** and introduces the knight to his son.

The father drafts the son to go to the knight. The boy, being the creditor in his father's draft, responds by walking over to the knight. The knight, being the beneficiary of the boy's father's draft (order) is now the creditor (title holder) of the young boy (the "res" of the draft).

The knight drafts the boy, asking: ***"Are you afraid of me, boy?"*** The lad, being the creditor of the knight's draft, responds and shakes his head, ***"No."***

The knight drafts him again and says: ***"Show me your teeth!"*** The boy obliges and the knight says in a third draft: ***"Show me an arm muscle!"*** The boy bends his arm and makes a fist and the knight is pleased.

The knight says to the father: ***"He's an about half***

starved little scarecrow, but he will do. He's got spirit."

The knight, who is now the creditor over the boy by way of the pledge of the father in the father's first draft, and by way of his acceptance of the father's offer, commands (drafts) the boy: ***"Go say good-by to your father."*** The boy carries out the draft command. The father who is now the creditor and beneficiary of the knight's draft, has creditor-ship over his son again and drafts him to say good-by.

After father and son good-bys, the father re-drafts his son to go back the knight. The knight is now the beneficiary of the father's drafts once again and he is the creditor who again holds title to the young boy.

The father gets into the boat and casts off.

The son runs to the water's edge and calls out: ***"Father?"*** The boys father says: ***"What?"*** The boy says: ***"I'm afraid... I don't know the way back home."*** The father says: ***"Follow your feet"*** and the boy returns to the knight.

Here we have perfect commercial harmony with all parties following their respective duties regarding honor to the other party. Here is a transaction by which the title to the boy changed hands from the father to the knight to the father and back again to the knight. The knight is now a creditor (title holder) of the young boy. The knight (as the boy's creditor) has responsibilities to the boy and the boy (as his debtor) has duties to the knight.

The father's answer to his son's inquiry about finding his way home is interesting. In life there are three aspect to one's actions — ***thought, word, and deed.*** In the end, it is the deed, or your actions that count.

One can *think* of going home and never get there. One can *talk* of going home and never get there. To get home requires the *action* of your deeds.

Maxim: **If one takes action there will be a way to overcome all obstacles to finding one's way home.**

If the boy is to "change his stars," then, "finding the way home" is not going back to the pauper's shack in London from whence he came. Home is following your feet to the goal you set for yourself when you want to change your stars.

Our young lad serves the knight for twelve years (a number representing perfect government). During this time he matures and the knight trains him to use the broad sword and to joust with lances. Now a young man, the boy was trained, in part, because the knight needed an opponent to train against when he was not touring in the tournaments, so that he could keep fit.

One day, in France, where the old knight had been competing in a minor tournament, the old knight dies during an intermission between jousts. Our young hero decides to put on the knight's armor and compete in the knight's place to win the prize money for himself and the knight's other two pages. He says: *"I'll ride in his place."* He finally talks the other two into going along with this effort because they need the prize money to by food — **an act of necessity.** They had not eaten in three days.

The young man wins the prize in the tournament by impersonating his master who had died. When the young man wins the tournament and gets the prize he splits the prize money with the other two page boys, and then talks them into continuing the ruse to compete in even bigger tournaments for more money that would meet their needs.

COMMERCIAL TRANSACTION WITH JOCELYN

After winning a number of tournaments in France, the young man — now known as Sir Ulrick van Lichtenstein of Geld-a-land — is getting a name for himself by his wins. He meets a beautiful young noblewoman named Jocelyn who follows the tournaments around France. She likes the young man. She tells her lady-in-waiting Christiana, that: **"He is the only knight that has not wooed me and said he would win the tournament and dedicate the win to my honor."**

One day that happens. The young man follows Jocelyn into a large church. He is trying to impress her. He says: **"I am going to win the tournament and dedicate it to your honor."** Jocelyn turns to the young man and says loudly: **"If you love me, you will lose the tournament, not win it."** The young man is stunned and confused... He angrily responds to her: **"It is no great feat to <u>lose</u> the tournament. It is a difficult task to <u>win</u> the tournament."**

A priest angrily approaches the young pair and yells to them both to **"Be quiet!"** (meaning, don't speak in the presence of God?)

The young man is upset. He leaves the church, and Jocelyn is the only party left standing in the church.

What just happened in these commercial transactions? Before we see the answer to that question, let's go to the Tournament to observe more regarding the above commercial transactions.

The Hidden Truth

Our young man is competing in the joust. He has his armor on and mounts his horse. He goes to the gates. His contest with his first opponent in this tournament begins. The young man does not charge his horse down the course. He stays in his position. His opponent charges him and with **no resistance** from the young man, knocks the young man nearly off his horse with a heavy blow from his lance.

The opponent has scored his first of three possible points.

For a second time, his opponent charges the young man. Again the young man stays **at rest** and is nearly knocked off his horse again. The young man's friends are very upset. They think that there must be something wrong. They ask the young man, what his problem is. The young man says: *"I love Jocelyn. She told me that if I love her, I should lose the tournament, not win it. I don't know why she said that, but I love her, so I will not win."*

Unknown to the young man, his friends have bet their whole savings on the young man to win this tournament. Therefore it appears that the tournament is a contest **between commerce** (money and bets) **and love.**

Nothing the young man's friends can say can get him to change his mind. Meanwhile, Jocelyn was in the stands observing what was going on. As the young man kept getting hit by the opponent's lance, every blow to the young man was like an arrow to her heart. She could not sit, but stood up and leaned against a column for support.

Finally, after the young man had deliberately lost two matches, his friends warned him that if he loses one more match, he will forfeit the tournament. Christiana comes to the young man and says: ***"My Lady said, If you love her, you should win the tournament."*** This was good news to the young man and his friends but it made him angry. The young knight goes on to win the tournament and dedicates it to Jocelyn.

Now again, what just happened?

Everything is commercial in nature. When something is commercial, the important thing is to find out, who is the **creditor** and who is the **debtor** in the procedure.

"Render therefore to all their dues: tribute to whom tribute is due; custom to whom custom; fear to whom fear; honor to whom honor." *— Romans 13:7.*

If one honors himself, he is making himself a creditor in the procedure. This appears to be a desirable goal, — but reality does not work this way. To make **yourself** a creditor is to act in the nature of pride. And we all know that pride comes before the fall. Pride is the condition of acting as the greatest one around.

When you set yourself up as a creditor you make all others debtors in the matter, with no capacity (energy) to act. They cannot participate with you in your self-appointed victory. One must always achieve greatness upon the ***voluntary*** declaration of others, by allowing them to be a creditor over you.

"Humble yourselves in the sight of the Lord, and he shall lift you up." *— James 4:10.*

The Hidden Truth

Jocelyn was upset with all the knights who promised that **she** would be honored upon their victory. Jocelyn knew that the knights are not honoring **her** as a creditor, but only **themselves**. There was nothing that she could do at the tournament that would help the knights win or lose. She knew that each knight who promised her this was using her as a prize with which to honor **himself**. She was therefore being made a **debtor** to the winning knight, with no capacity to act.

This was no honor to lady Jocelyn. Any knight who would make that offer to her was attempting to **buy** her favor as though she were merely an object to be bought.

When the young man made her the same promise in the church, Jocelyn was upset because he had been honoring her as a **creditor** who could act, up until that time. The young man had always treated her as a woman of honor and a creditor on a *quid pro quo* (honor for honor) basis with him. To offer to make her the object of his honor, as a token of him winning the tournament, was to dishonor her.

She tried to tell him why she was upset. He would not listen.

The priest who yelled at them: *"Be quiet!"* upset Jocelyn. **The true church is there to train people up in The Law.** True law requires that we honor those to whom honor is due. Jocelyn was trying to tell the young man what the substance of the law really is.

Jocelyn re-drafted the priest in such a way that the priest did not have an answer, and he walked away losing the commercial contact with her. The young man also walked away, losing the battle with her, at that time, since he did not understand Jocelyn's position and did not know what to say to her — so he **stood mute,** in default.

When the young man went to the tournament and lost the first two matches, he **honored** Jocelyn's draft. Remember, she said: *"If you love me, you will lose."* So the young man **honored** Jocelyn's draft by forfeiting the first two matches, then Joceyln re-drafted him to win.

By **honoring** her and winning the tournament, the young man now won Jocelyn's heart by making her the creditor (with commercial power) behind his winning of the tournament. They were now **both** on a *quid quo pro* basis and were **both** creditors having power to perform.

This example of "commercial transactions" is one of several examples you will find in the movie, *"The Knight's Tale."*

26
The London Joust

The young hero in the movie **"A Knight's Tale"** was warned by his friends that if he was caught impersonating a knight, he would be imprisoned for life. After all, **"Knight"** was a Title of Nobility set forth by an act of the king. Impersonating the King's titles was a felony.

By the time we get to the final tournament of the Summer in the movie, the knights are back in England, in London. Our young hero has come home for the first time since his father had placed him in the care of his mentor, an old knight — twelve years ago.

Before the tournament, the young man goes to the lower side of London to see if his father might still be there after all this time. He finds his father still there, but the young man's arch enemy — a jealous knight named Count Ademar of Anjure — follows him and learns that he is not of noble birth. Count Ademar reports him to the credentials committee of the tournament charging him with impersonating a knight.

When the young man shows up at the tournament the next morning to compete, he is informed by this friends that there is a warrant out for his arrest for impersonating a knight. They warn him that if he competes in the tournament he will be arrested by the sheriff, taken away in chains, convicted, and placed in the dungeon for the rest of his life.

All of the young man's friends order him not to compete in the tournament. This is a commercial draft.

His friends are the drawers of the draft. His friends

are debtors and he is a creditor in the procedure. The obligation to respond is his, and he must make a timely decision. To sit back and do nothing is to eventually be arrested anyway.

The young man asks questions of his friends. Asking questions is always a safe thing to do when one is in doubt. Their consensus is that nothing practical would come out of his going to the tournament and getting arrested. There is no way that the young man could refute the charges in the King's court. He is guilty of impersonating the King's knight with no proof of knight-hood being given to him by the king. He would merely be throwing away his future life and potential for no good gain.

The young man asks Jocelyn, his lover, who is also there: **"What about our relationship?"** Jocelyn responds that she will love him no matter what, title or not, or what name he has. She will go away with him and live with him for who he is.

"Oh! Jocelyn, you speak of what you do not know! responds the young man.

The young man says to her that eventually she will hate him, because she will never be able to live a life of luxury and peace again by following him while he is a fugitive from the justice. To which one of the young man's friend says: **"You have the ability to compete and win over the best of the knights — but you do not have a title."**

The young man finally declares:

"No! I will not run! I am a knight. I will put myself to the hazard. I will go to the tournament and compete."

What is so different between many of the patriots

today and the young man who claims he is a knight?

In the real world — in the *private* sector — the young man was better than most of the King's official knights. The only problem was that the *public* sector is run by the king, under the king's rules; and in the *public* sector it is necessary that your **"paper work"** be in order according to the king's officers.

"Show me your papers please."

As an example, you might be the best driver of an automobile in the state. You might be courteous and give honor to all the other drivers on the road. But if you do not have a "driver's license" (a commercial document) issued by the king, then the public servants of the king (law enforcement officers and the king's agents) will not **"see"** you as a driver and will charge you with a statutory violation, on the road.

It is not a real world of reason and truth. It is a world of **the king's paper and titles.** Documents and **recognition** are all that count. Without a document that states which domain you live in, you have no **evidence** that you are in the private domain. Without **"patents of nobility,"** you are a peasant impersonating a knight.

COMMERCIAL PROCESS & WARRANTS OF ARREST

Maxim: You must go low to be make high.

The young man is informed by his friends that a warrant has been issued for his arrest. What is an arrest warrant? It is simply a draft.

Usually an informer or an agent of the king goes to the king's prosecutor and fills out an **"Information"** wherein the charging party alleges that the accused committed some act in violation of the king's statutes.

This **"Information"** is a draft in the prosecutor's hands [**draft #1**]. The charging party is the ***drawer*** of this draft and the prosecutor is its ***creditor***.

The charging party is the ***debtor*** *[who is low]* and the prosecutor is the ***creditor*** *[who is in control]* at this point. The *ball [credit]* is in the prosecutor's hands, energizing him to perform.

The prosecutor goes to the king's magistrate and drafts him to issue an arrest warrant. This is a second and separate draft [**draft #2**].

The prosecutor is the ***drawer*** of draft #2 and the magistrate is its ***drawee***.

The magistrate is now the ***creditor*** *[who is in control]* who is energized to issue the arrest-warrant. The magistrate may or may not ask the prosecutor to show **"probable cause"** for him to authorize the arrest. If the magistrate requires it, **"probable cause"** would be a redraft of draft #2.

Assuming that the magistrate is satisfied, he issues the arrest warrant [**draft #3**] against the accused. This draft orders one of the king's law enforcement officers to arrest the accused and bring him before the king's court.

The magistrate is the ***drawer*** of draft #3 and the king's law enforcement officer is its ***drawee***. This makes the king's law enforcement officer the ***creditor*** *[who is control]* who is empowered to arrest the accused.

The king's officer who locates the accused approaches him with the warrant for his arrest. ***"Are you (and he names your strawman's name)?"*** This is

draft #4 drafting the accused to respond. The officer is **drawer** of draft #4 and the accused is the **drawee**. This makes the officer the **debtor** *[who is low]* and the accused the **creditor!...who is now in control!**

Bet you never expected the officer to be *honoring* the accused by asking his name, making him the **creditor...who is now in control!**

At this stage of the game in the process there are some interesting procedures that must be followed if you want to get it right, because the warrant names your all-capital-lettered strawman's name.

You have two choices. **Honor or dishonor.** The only way **to honor draft #4** is to **accept it and re-draft.**

One should comply, and say: *"YES I am, and I order you to take me before the court AT ONCE!"*

By accepting the offer for your arrest, you are the **creditor** *[who is in control]* of the transaction including the original charge. This whole process is procedural. It has nothing to do with right or wrong; it is to get you to appear before the court to answer the charge for your strawman.

Your draft to the law enforcement officer [**draft #5**], to take you before the court **"AT ONCE!"** energizes the officer by making him the **creditor** *[who is in control]* who must act on your draft or be in default. If he fails to carry out your order — your order to take you before the court **"AT ONCE!"** — he is in dishonor and the roles are reversed. he needs to be put on notice by a **Notarial Protest** that he has dishonored your draft [**draft #5**].

To be the winner in a commercial charge one has to end up as the **creditor** *[who is in control]*.

To charge the officer with breach of duty, one has to allege a duty under **draft #5**, and its subsequent dishonor, which can only be shown with a **Notarial Protest** issued against the officer for breaching his duty under **draft #5** to take you **"before the court AT ONCE!"**

This makes the accused the *creditor* [*who is in control*] under his draft [**draft #5**] and empowers him to bring charges against the officer.

If the officer was not timely drafted by the accused to *"take me before the court AT ONCE!"* and if the officer is not issued a timely **Notarial Protest** upon his failure to honor that draft, then the accused *"fails to state a claim upon which relief can be granted"* by not showing evidence of his status as the *creditor* [*who is in control*] at the end.

Once the accused is before the magistrate the accused is still the *creditor who is in control* of the original charge (**draft #1**) that is charging his strawman with the *informer's* alleged charge. Drafts #2, #3, #4, and #5 are relevant to the procedure only).

What the accused does at this point is critical to his remaining in honor or his falling into dishonor. **Status is the only relevant thing.** Innocence or guilt, right or wrong, facts and allegations, are not important now. **Status is the only thing that matters in the end.**

The accused must *"Accept the charge* [**draft #1**] *for value on the condition of proof"* and not *resist, argue, or ignore the charge* (to avoid dishonor).

The accused must then *redraft* the charges to get the ball out of his court without dishonor taking place. The redraft must be **an order for some response** that will raise an estoppel to the proceedings without a court order being carried out.

A typical redraft might be, *"I accept the charges for value on the condition that you prove your authority over me."*

In other words, *"I request that the order of the court be released to me at once."*

This is a perfect redraft.

You have now moved the ball into the plaintiff's court and he is again the **creditor** *[who is in control]*. As the creditor, the plaintiff now has the duty to prove his claim. Can he do it? Probably not if he is from the public side. The public is a **debtor** and a debtor can not have title — unless you give it to him.

You either gave it to him already, or the public is seeking to get it from you. In any event:

Maxim: **He who alleges a fact must prove it.**

This requires the **plaintiff** to prove the thing, not the **accused** unless the accused dishonors the plaintiff's draft [**draft #1**]. Facts argued in the court are immaterial. An accused loses his case, of his own accord if he dishonors the claim, whether he is right or not.

OUR HERO CHANGES HIS STARS

The young man who declared: *"I am a knight!"* understood that he had to compete in the tournament and act like a knight, even though there was a warrant out for his arrest.

To flee would be to dishonor the king's warrant.

By being named in the arrest warrant the young man is the **drawee** and a **creditor** *[who is in control]*. To run away would make him a debtor by his **volun-**

tary dishonor of the charge.

The young man's father had said to him, when he was just a lad: *"You can change your stars."*

The young man started out as a pauper. He was a **debtor** then. That is all he would ever be in the service of the king in the public domain if he did not *"change his stars."* To avoid the warrant and run away would be equivalent to remaining a **debtor** forever and his stars would never change.

To the young man, his **"home"** was the condition of **"changing his stars"** — to become a **creditor** instead of a **debtor**. To do this, he had to face the charges and show that he was a man of honor; *a true knight.*

To be a knight is to be a man of honor in deed. The young man could **think** like a man of honor. He could **speak** like a man of honor. But only by **being** a man of honor in deed could he be a real knight.

But for the **public** to accept him as a knight required **the public witness of others** to make him in fact a real knight. His **private claim** had to be brought before the king's **public domain** to be seen.

Jocelyn (his royal-bride-to-be) can be seen as a metaphor for the **Church of Christ.** Christ's church is not a building, not a 501(c)3 corporation, nor a religious institution. Jocelyn was not the corporate church.

The priest in the corporate church was only interested in the **form** of the **execution of law** — *in remaining silent and not making waves*. Jocelyn wanted to see the true substance of understanding and following the law, not simply procedural agreement.

When the young man asked his friends what they

would have him do with respect to the warrant, even Jocelyn said that he should flee. She would go with him of course. This is the first time that Jocelyn did not give good advice to the young man she loved. But to honor him she could not tell him to *not* do what he had to do. The young man represents the Christ. By letting the young man make the decision, the church took second place before God.

The church (typified by Jocelyn) had seen the boy grow from a servant to a man of honor; a man of God. The church stepped back, so he would step into lawful government as a Man of Honor who followed the law.

The young man goes to the tournament and is arrested. He accepts full responsibility for the charge. He does not argue a defense by debating the charges. His friends stand by him and by their actions testify to the public that the accused is a man of honor. This is **a third-party witness**, not the witness of oneself.

Now comes a Proclamation by the son of the king regarding the honor that the young man showed by his actions (not by his words). Prince Edward, the Black Prince of Wales who had been watching from the crowd, came forward and began to speak:

"What a pair we make! Both trying to hide who we are, and not able to do so. Your men love you. If I knew nothing else about you, that would be enough. You also tilt when you should withdraw, and that is knightly too.

"Release him.

"He may appear to be of humble origins but my personal historians have discovered that he is a descendent from an ancient royal line... (he is a child of God). ***This is my word, and as such is beyond contestation.***

Then again to William. *"If I may repay the kindness that you once showed me... take a knee...*

"In the power vested in me by King Edward... and by the witnesses here... I dub thee, Sir William the Thatcher... Arise, Sir William..."

This Royal Proclamation by the king's son created a *public acceptance* of newly knighted Sir William Thatcher, by the operation of law. His **private claim** was now recognized in the **public domain**. He changed his stars after all.

He followed his feet... He found his way home.

27
The Real Game In Town

It's not FOOTBALL [code violations, truth, or law], it's HOCKEY [honor or dishonor]!

And we wonder why we're being knocked around. We've fallen prey to the myths of the day, to the fantasies de jure...that courtrooms do not operate on the truth, the law, or the facts. Ah, but they do.

We lose when we have the truth, the law, and the facts on our side, like slipping on thin ice.

The game has been hockey all along, and we come in, in shoulder pads, helmets, and cleats, fully prepared to argue the facts and the law — all the legal reasons why the judge should rule in our favor. In defense of our case. But we lose just the same.

Well, the cat's now out of the bag. Now we know how to interpret the rules of the game — AND THE SCORE! Just bring the court a stipulation. Place the judge in his ministerial capacity where he sheds his mantle of judicial immunity!

Our first sense of knowing how to interpret the victories came from a guy who was with me when we overheard two attorneys go through this scenario in a courtroom:

Woman attorney: "Your honor, he hasn't responded to my letters or my phone calls." **Interpretation:** Your honor, he's in dishonor by his silence.

Man attorney: "Your honor, she's just trying to start an argument." **Interpretation:** I want to argue that she's arguing; I don't know any other way to be in dishonor and lose.

Woman attorney: "Your honor, he hasn't even responded to my phone call of this past Friday." **Interpretation:** Your honor, he has a pattern of dishonor.

Judge: "Now, now. I don't see why I shouldn't hear his arguments." **Interpretation:** Come on, children, you both know that the whole system is set up so I get discretion over all your presumptions because no one can prove anything and that's how we all keep our jobs and charge our clients higher court-appearance fees. If I start letting it be known that I choose who loses on your dishonors, the game would be over and none of us would have work.

The judge to the woman: "Would you re-submit your case cites?" **Interpretation:** Can't we get back on track and start the arguments again and forget this honor-dishonor stuff even though I know you know what to do; but not why. Case cites are arguments (dishonors). They are nothing but opinions and presumptions that are public illusions.

The woman obviously didn't know the "why" so she said "Yes, sir", and we were back inside the box where the cat can't be described in the dark.

On the way home, my friend commented: "Now that you explained that interpretation to me, I see why judges never read any more than one or two pages of each of the briefs of each side, no matter how long the briefs are or how many case cites you put in, or how much evidence you attach."

Brilliant, my friend, I said. Absolutely brilliant. Just another clue in the "hide-in-plain-sight" remedy that we were never taught.

UNTIL NOW!

Now we know that nothing matters, not the truth, the facts or the law, especially not the law that we ignorantly use to beat them over the head and shoulders with, going into dishonor and permitting them to ignore the truth, the law, and the facts.

28
Public v. Private

There are only two types of jurisdiction in the world today; the Public v. the Private.

You are a private body because you exist there; everything outside you is public.

The "sweat and blood" of the Bible refers to both jurisdictions. Sweat is "public," outside. Blood is "private," inside.

Blood is a private flowing that gives life. All rights come from your right to privacy. In the private sector, everybody minds his own business. In the public sector, everyone tends to the business of someone else.

Public court is a waste of your time. It is futile to raise constitutional rights in the contract courts of today. The public has no final remedy because you're asking executors of law to fix what you should fix yourself. In executions of law something has to die.

You are the biggest problem to yourself. You have to be straight in order to exercise a remedy that will last. Only you can provide your remedy. Don't ask the public to save you from yourself. Remedy can only be found in the private domain.

You are the solution to your problems. Your private existence is where you make the judgment call. Your internal jurisdiction is the private domain, not the papers you file in a court.

Your view is the dividing line between the public and private domain. It is all according to how you perceive things of your own accord. Just because you say it is private doesn't necessarily make it so. It's how you operate your life that makes it so.

When things enter the public domain they spin out of control due to the spiral of public debt. Releasing information into the public domain corrupts it because the public can't cope with the liberties that come with a private knowledge of the law. There's a veil over their hearts. This is why Jesus spoke in parables. Only those who are supposed to understand at a particular time, will.

Moses first brought down the higher Law of the private side. But when he saw the people worshipping the golden calf, he knew it would have been a liability on his head if he were to disseminate the higher Law to the public in his day. So he went back up the Mount and returned with the Mosaic Law for the public. That was all the public could bear at that time. Too many liberties wreak havoc on a people not prepared to accept the freedoms liberty entails.

The golden rule ("Do unto others as you would have them do unto you") sums up all private thought. The private sector requires the discernment of Mind.

If you owe anyone money you are public. The private owes nobody anything as they are the source of the money (**credit**) owed.

When someone presents you with a bill (an order for money from your strawman is a money order for you) **he has to give you a remedy.** As the accepting party, you must be able to pass through his name (his **credit**) for the energy of your remedy to be released.

A check is a three part instrument. You [A] are telling the bank [B] to pay C. This is a Pass-through account. The bank uses **your name** (**your credit**) as the creator of the funds to provide the money (**credit**) to be moved from B to C. And this cannot be done unless you are the bridge (the transmitting utility between them) that provides the **credit** from your account.

When a person dishonors and won't produce his "offer" to provide your remedy, after your "acceptance of the adjustment of the account" for "the adjustment of the account," he loses his exemption (due to his dishonor) until he settles up with you. He loses his exemption because he won't let your credit pass through his account for him to get paid.

When you get a letter either demanding something from you or an acceptance letter of an action you've presented to someone else — both of which are trying to use **your name** to get some benefit from you — you need to accept it.

When you accept the claim made against you, return it to the sender so that it will pay for itself.

Because we live under public policy, we are not obligated to pay. The most we can do is accept the charge and return it back on itself to pay for itself, because this is the remedy public policy allows.

When you accept an offer, the offeror must allow your credit to pass-through his account by his acceptance of your acceptance. When he has done this, he has accepted a bill drawn against him and returned it to you for negotiation.

Now that both parties have accepted what has happened, neither party owes each other anything because the original acceptor returned the claim for full settlement, and the offeror accepted the return so the debt has been effectively redeemed.

When a party continues to dishonor, he is not allowing his exemption to pay for your return, so he loses his private exemption and becomes public. When a presenter does not settle with you he becomes liable for the public debt he created. It is all based upon public policy insurance.

The bottom-line is that "We cannot be obligated to pay a debt; <u>the most we are obligated to do</u> is to "make-right" the payment, which means <u>accept and return</u>.

We must to do all that we can — <u>accept and return</u>. Then mercy steps in, being Grace. Your exemption covers the payment for you. Your inability to pay covers it instead; the same as Grace.

Everything outside of your body is the Industrial Society. **It is all "public works":** - "the system" - "government" - "commerce" - "proprietors" - "trusts" - "banks" - "license holders" - "titles of nobility" - "manufactures" - "the courts" - "mutual funds" - "stocks and bonds" - "your friends" - "nightclubs" - and the like.

It is all the "industrial society".

29
New World Order? Or Release

"Choose ye this day whom ye will serve." — Joshua 24:15.

The biblical regathering of Israel began in America in 1776. This involved three 70-year periods of servitude to the world because of our Founding Fathers pledged America's assets to the British Crown.

By mortgaging God's people to creditors in Europe, they rejected God as their ruler and king once again.

Even so, we can set ourselves free from America's debt to the Crown, on an individual basis. Why? Because we've reached the crossroads of three periods of bondage to the "kings of this world".

To drive the British troops off American soil, and to keep afloat during the American Revolutionary War, the Confederate States borrowed money from the Crown, and the Peace treaty of 1872 extended the loans for six years.

When Congress foresaw that they couldn't pay back the debt when it became due in 1788, they convened the Constitutional Convention of 1787 to establish a **"constitutum"**.

To resolve their dilemma, Congress **constituted the states of America** to agree to pay its existing debt to the Crown, and Congress has been indebted to the Crown ever since.

The Confederacy that had signed for the loans made

the **states of America** liable for the debt (its co-signers) so the creditor's wouldn't call the loan.

The Constitution was devised to give the Crown in England a **"mortgage"** on the otherwise new so-called **"free states"**.

The states mortgaged their future, via the Constitution, when it was ratified in 1789. The states sold their inheritance of freedom for a mess of pottage, and incurred a 70-year penalty for their default on the debt.

CONSTITUTUM: **"an agreement to pay ones own or another's existing debt."** (*Blacks Law 7th, page 307*).

CONSTITUTOR: **"a person who, by agreement, becomes responsible for another's debt."** (*ibid*).

The **"Law of Servitude"** regarding master and slave applies to the biblical **"year of release"** when a servant is to be set free. But if a servant loves his master and desires to continue serving him, the freed servant could voluntarily enter into servitude to his master again. See **Exodus 21:2-6** regarding **voluntary servitude**.

So the United States voluntarily became a servant again of the Crown for three periods of seventy years.

1. The first period of seventy years takes us to **the first Year of release and the Civil War** (**1859**) when the mortgage was not released but instead renewed. **The Civil War** prepared the people for the government takeover of the states that had become accommodation parties to its debts.

2. The second period of seventy years takes us to **the second Year of release and the Great Depres-**

sion (**1929**) when the mortgage was not released but instead renewed. **The Great Depression** prepared the people for the socialization of America. The states had no assets when the ongoing mortgage was called, so Congress **pledged public assets of the people** to the public domain, so the public could borrow funds to support itself and make payments on its loans, **via Roosevelt's 1933 "New Deal".**

3. The third period of seventy years takes us to **the third Year of release and the Clinton impeachment trial** (1999). **The Clinton impeachment trial** was a silent referendum for the nation to decide if it wanted to **"come out"** from the mortgage or **"stay in"** bankruptcy to the Crown, and join the **New World Order** begun in 1933 when the mortgage was renewed.

The nation chose to **"stay in"** slavery to the national debt, so it's playing out its part in the **One World-Government** of today.

But Congress had to give each member of the U.S. Corporation the opportunity to *"come out from among them and be separate"* and no longer be liable for Congress and its debt.

We can choose (individually) to *"come out from among them and be separate"* via CPR, and be responsible for ourselves. This is what **commercial redemption** is about.

"Come out from among them, and be ye separate, and touch not the unclean thing." — 2 Corinthians 6:17.

30
Redemption & The Lord's Release

America's War for independence from Great Britain that began 1776 was settled per the Treaty of Peace in Paris, France in 1783.

To finance this War of Independence from the King, the continental Congress borrowed money from the Crown. 3,000,000 livres in 1778. 1,000,000 livres in 1779. 4,000,000 livres in 1780. And 6,000,000 livres in 1782. A total of 18,000,000 livres in all.

On July 16, 1782, Benjamin Franklin, Esq. signed a treaty, **a mortgage loan agreement under international law** with the King of France — establishing the following:

1) a creditor,
2) a debtor,
3) consideration,
4) specific performance on the debt,
5) the opportunity for others (such as ourselves) to help pay for the loan (hence our presumed liability for that debt).

The loan was for six years, due and payable on the first of January, 1789 and Congress defaulted on the loan, placing the new nation into bankruptcy to the Crown.

The main reason for the constitutional convention and, the American Constitution at that time, was to amend the Articles of Confederation to include the obligation for this loan.

The Constitution was ratified on September 13, 1788, 6 weeks prior to the default on the loan, disguising the bankruptcy of the United States to the Crown.

CONSTITUTOR: A person who by agreement becomes responsible for another's debt. (Blacks Law 7th, p.307).

Four years later, in 1791, George Washington established the National Bank of the United States, under emergency law rule, as a private bank to hold the securities of the bankrupt United States for the Crown.

When the bank's charter expired 20 years later in 1811 it was not renewed, so England used military force to attack the United States in the War of 1812, and burn the Capital Building and the White House in order to destroy the original 13th Amendment and to have the Crown's securities restored under international law.

Therefore, a second National Bank of the United States was established in 1816 to provide securities to the Crown for Congress' defaulted loan.

The principles of international law are dictated by public international law and the law of nations, one interesting aspect of which is the law that deals with captivity, bondage, redemption, and release.

"At the end of every seven years thou shalt make a release. Every creditor that lendeth ought unto his neighbor shall release it. Because it is called the Lord's release." — Deuteronomy 15:1,2.

"And these nations shall serve the king of Babylon seventy years." — Jeremiah 25:11.

The Lord's release for **man** is every 7 years; and

for **nations** ten times 7 years, or 70 years.

For example, the Captivity of the Juda-ites in Babylon lasted for 70 years; from 607 B.C. to 537 B.C.

Jacob served his father-in-law Laban for 21 years — 7 years as an apprentice, 7 years as a dowry for his wife Leah, and 7 years as a dowry for his wife Rachel — a total of 21 years. After 21 years his time was his own.

After 21 years Jacob was set free from his economic contract with his father-in-law. This 21 year period is known as **"Jacob's Trouble"**.

Captivity for man is 7 years; and for nations ten times 7 years or 70 years.

There is a **short captivity** — such as the 70 year captivity of the Judaites of Daniel's time in Babylon, and the 70 year captivity of the Soviet Union as a communist nation in our time — and a **long captivity** — such as the 210 year captivity of God's People in Egypt, in Moses time, prior to the Exodus.

The greater captivity for **man** is 21 years (3 x 21 = 70), and the greater captivity for **nations** is ten times 21 years or 210 years. The Children of Israel were subject to Egypt for 210 years before God set them free through Moses.

The United States went into captivity under international economic law for 210 years, just as the Children of Israel did under Egypt in Jeremiah's time.

When we add 210 years to the first loan default date of January 1, 1789, we get January 1, 1999 — the year of release for the American colonies, under international law, from the bankruptcy of the United States that resulted from Congress' loans of 1789.

When dealing in bankruptcy, an individual can go through bankruptcy and have his debts declared "discharged" and then turn around and **renew** his obligation for the debt by an operation of law. The law will then require that the person pay the discharged debt even though it had been discharged in the bankruptcy.

This procedure was used in 1999 to get the American people to renew the corporate debt of the United States to the Crown of England during its time of release from that debt under international law. The **second** 13th Amendment to the Constitution permits "voluntary servitude" — and Exodus 21:5 allows a servant to voluntarily serve his master after his release in the **"Year of release."**

Most of our legislators in Washington, D.C. are Esquire attorneys who work for the Crown whether they know it or not.

Let's assume that they know that the United States is in Chapter 11 bankruptcy to the Crown, and that the year of the Lord's release is up so that the United States can elect to have its national debt discharged and its sovereign status as a republic restored, instead of being the democracy it now is.

This means that the tax collections, for the past 70 years, to pay back the debt to the Crown, would expire — unless the United States renewed its debt to the Crown.

Let's assume that the attorney and politicians did not want to tell the people that an option to stop paying on the national debt to the Crown existed in this "Year of release." However, under international law, both parties must be informed of their options if their agreement is to be altered or renewed.

Under international law, the Crown of England and its agents had to inform the American people of the law that entitled them to be released from the nations debt to the Crown and be free.

Thence the question: How could the Crown of England and its esquire agents in D.C. tell us that the United States could elect to have its national debt discharged in the "Year if release" (1999) in such a way that we would not catch on to that fact?

Let's assume that the attorneys of the Crown (and its principals including the Vatican) establish a **"great debate"** to decide whether or not the people of the United States want to leave their servitude and be free.

Let's assume that the **"great debate"** will be such that no living soul in the land could escape the debate and its conclusive decision. All must know about it. It must be the talk of the town throughout the land. It must involve great principles at the highest level of the law.

Let's assume that the vehicle chosen for the debate would distract the American people from the true intent and meaning of the debate. What kind of a **"great debate"** would we, as agents of the Crown, choose?

I know!

Let's charge the President of the United States with a crime!

Of course, we're not really interested in what the president might do to commit the crime; the real issue would be the **procedure** that we would use to bring this issue before the American people.

The attorney and politicians would pretend that they

don't know what procedure they should use. They would refer that question to the American people, as to what to do, in a presidential criminal trial.

Under what **law form (venue)** is the president to be tried?

If the president is accused of some criminal offense, then he must be tried by some form of tribunal, but Which one? The nation has been a **military democracy** for many years. A democracy is a military government that is ruled in an emergency by a commander-in-chief. In a democracy the people are not free. They are the subjects of a democratic law form.

If a nation wants to be released from captivity it must revert from a **military democracy** back to a **republic at peace**, and leave its commercial bondage behind.

The people should have insisted that the rules of the Clinton Impeachment trial be set in the **republic law form** of a sovereign nation, under the original Constitution FOR the United States of 1789. Under a **republican law form** a president can be impeached.

If the nation wants to renew its debt to the international bankers and the Crown, after the **"Year of release,"** it must continue under a **democratic law form** under which the commander-in-chief is sovereign and cannot be touched by the people under his charge.

The people should have insisted that the rules of the Clinton Impeachment trial be set in the **democratic law form** of a military nation, under the de facto Constitution OF the United States of 1891. Under a **democratic law form** the commander-in-chief can never be impeached, because his rule is law, he can only be sanctioned in his public capacity as president.

The American people were being asked to vote, by a national referendum, on whether the nation was to become free, or continue as subjects to the king and the international bankers who are foreign to the United States. The notion that President Clinton had committed a crime, was the **vehicle** for the debate, not its **subject**.

Since there was no lawful **"Notice of Protest,"** the old law form remained in effect. Since there was no lawful **"Notice of Protest"** before the Senate voted for the democracy, and against impeachment, the law form of the bankruptcy, and our debtor enslavement to the English Crown continues in force.

"Now these are the judgments that thou shalt set before them. If thou buy an Hebrew servant (this is what happened when we were sold into bankruptcy)*, six years shall he serve: and in the seventh he shall go out free for nothing* (this was the national release in the seventh year)*, [but] if the servant shall plainly say, "I love my master. . . I will not go out free: Then his master shall bring him unto the judges* (this was the result of the "great debate")*; he shall also bring him to the door, or unto the door post; and his master shall bore his ear through with an aul; and he shall serve him for ever."* — Exodus 21:1,2,5.

The practice of placing an earring in an ear is the practice of branding one as a slave to his master under voluntary consent. Hence the significance of an earring in the ear; the symbol of the slave.

The William Jefferson Clinton Impeachment Trial was about voluntary consent. It had nothing to do with the accusations involved. It had nothing to do with whether he was guilty or not. It dealt with the **"rules of procedure"** upon which the trial was to be conducted. By not choosing the rules of a republic, we chose the law form for the triers of the case. We chose the wrong law form, and kept the democracy in force. We said, **"We will not go free."**

There has never been a real impeachment process of any President of the United States since our nation was founded, because the United States has been under bankruptcy to the Crown of England since the Revolutionary War.

We are in breach of an international treaty when we trade with the Crown's corporate holdings in the United States. By engaging in the King's commerce in this way, we are **"converting to our own use"** assets of the British Crown, resulting in the Crown's rulership over us. We are being held accountable for a loan that came due more than 200 years ago in 1789.

The creditor is the head, and the debtor is the tail. The United States has been a British Colony since that time.

Wake up, America. It's always darkest before the dawn. Even though the bankruptcy of the United States has been renewed, you can still have your part in the forgiveness of the national debt as a result of the Lord's Release, through the Redemption in Law process, per HJR-192 and UCC 3-419.

EPILOGUE:

After the depression of 1908, the United States negotiated with the international bankers, to which its debt was again in default; at J.P. Morgan's vacation retreat, at Jekyll Island, Georgia, in the fall of 1910.

The United States was given a 20 year moratorium on paying its debt to the Crown of England in exchange for its promise to permit the establishment of a third private, central bank (the Federal Reserve) in which would be deposited the securities of the nation as sureties on its unpaid debt.

Twenty years later, the United States defaulted again. This default caused the stock market collapse of 1929, when the United States was reorganized under chapter 11 of the bankruptcy once again, putting its citizens under the unpaid debt that according to international law made them again captive servants of the Crown.

The citizens of the United States went into captivity under international economic law like the Children of Israel in Jeremiah's time.

31
The Passover

"Passover" (exchanging a past liability for a future liability) gives you the option to accept the charge (the salvation offered by Christ) by allowing it to pass over [pass through] your return — an action of the freewoman in accordance with public policy, which is Grace.

Treasury bills are for past liabilities of one year or less; **Treasury notes** are for present liabilities; **Treasury bonds** are for future labilities of ten years or more.

Notes insure bills, and bonds insure both notes and bills. A greater debt insures a lesser debt.

By calling directly upon the execution of law, by submitting a bill as though the law is a bond, the offeror turns the bill into a bond that exchanges the past liability for a future liability, and this exchange discharges the present liability of the bill, **whereby the offeror indebts himself for the value of his claim by dishonoring public policy, which is Grace** thus discharging the note for the acceptor of the charge, thereby grounding the charge to zero.

Public policy is the supersedeas bond. The bond that supersedes (overrides) all other bonds.

All contracts have to be in accord with public policy. Public policy removes the obligation to make payment in money. Public policy makes our payment for us by discharging the charge **when we accept the charge** that Christ discharged for us as the offered salvation of Christ.

The bill is exchanged for a bond against the drawer (the presenter) when it is presented in disregard of public policy.

The presenter is **converted** from a creditor to a debtor by his disregard of **public policy** (which is a manifestation of the Christ).

We need to determine who is entitled to the offer to determine who will get the blessing. In our society, two jurisdictions are intertwined, the jurisdiction of the **free-woman,** and the jurisdiction of the **bond-maid.**

We choose which jurisdiction we are in, public policy (HJR-192) or private equity law.

The bond-maid is of Mt. Sinai (the public domain of Mosaic law) and free-woman is of Christ (the private domain of Christ). The difference between the two is the ACCEPTANCE of **public policy** (Christ) — the discharge of the account.

"Forgive us our debts, as we forgive our debtors." — Matthew 6:12.

When you accept Christ, your are now of the **free-woman**; no longer of the **bond-maid**. The promise (the note; the entitlement) goes to the acceptor of the offeror's promise to deliver the goods. The acceptor is entitled to the delivery of what the offeror offers to him. The acceptor is entitled to the promise which is the value of the note.

The note is the offerer's promise to deliver the promised goods.

"Think not to say within yourselves, We have Abraham to our father: for I say unto you, that God is able of these stones to raise up children unto Abraham." — Matthew 3:9.

Our fiduciaries act like they are entitled to the promise, when in fact it takes an acceptance of the charge, — acceptance of Christ's forgiveness (write-off) of the account — for that to happen.

The promise consists of all the goods and services necessary for our existence in Christ's straight and narrow way.

When the offerer doesn't pay for his demand, by providing a check to pay the value of his claim, he is treating me as though my credit is the bond he is drawing against. He is attempting to make a withdrawal from my exemption, instead of his, He is overdrafting the value of his demand without giving anything in return.

The moment the offerer billed me (past liability) without providing me with a promissory note (present liability; a check), he drew on my credit as though I were the bond (future liability). He "passed over" the note by calling upon my bond to pay my strawman, thus paying the bill and the note by the bond.

Public policy reverses the entries so that the offeror who acts in disregard of public policy becomes a child of the bond-maid. By not forgiving me *my* debt, his debts won't be forgiven *him*.

Acceptance in accordance with public policy allows the debt to **"pass over"** me back to the offerer who now becomes a bond-maid's child.

Because he didn't free me of my bondage, he's not freed of the bondage he placed on himself. By claiming me to be his debtor, he indebted himself to me; he indebted himself for the value of my debt to him. Again:

"Forgive us our debts, as we forgive our debtors." — Matthew 6:2.

"Be ye kind to one another, tender-hearted, for-

giving one another even as God for Christ's sake hath forgiven you." — Ephesians 4:32.

The offeror indebted himself to me because public policy (my bond) makes it against public policy to make a payment in debt and draws a value equal to that made against me (the accepter) against him, because he **"passed over"** the note and failed to give me his check for the value of his claim. i.e., the **credit** for the initial production of the goods.

When the bill **"passed over"** the note, it moved from the past to the present for settlement, into the future calling the bond due. A bond is a debt instrument that cannot pay a debt.

My accuser is calling upon me as though I am a bondmaid child. **He is treating me as his debtor instead of the initial sponsor of the credit of the note.** He bypassed the promissory note and began to execute me for payment instead.

The promissory note represents the blessings in the storehouse. It represents the material goods that we need to survive.

A creditor only has to show a debtor on his books to make his vendor's check good. He doesn't even have to have money in the account.

When a holder-in-due-course holds an instrument (like a check) he can draw on the account, even when no money is in the account, even when no overdraft protection exists.

Labelling you as a debtor, the accuser has put you to death (into debt) or is trying to execute you. Public policy is our **supersedeas bond** that stops the execution and makes the payment in our behalf by transforming the liability back to the person that demanded money without providing his credit for the expenditure. When the Promise is **"passed over"**, the offeror becomes a bondmaid's child.

The **corporation** (the offeror) has promised to pay the note (the blessing) to the acceptor who then owns the note because the corporation is the maker of the offer (the note). The **corporation** has the liability to deliver the offering because that is the purpose it serves. **Corporations** make offers hoping they won't be accepted.

When the offer is not delivered, but withheld, the **corporation** becomes a delinquent holder of the blessing after the account has been accepted and is entitled to be released.

When the release is refused, the **corporation** becomes a tax fugitive because he is "withholding the offer" (and its liability). The order for adjustment (my acceptance) is an off-book asset, and their failure to apply it to zero-out the account, creates a tax delinquency on their part. They are holding **off-book energy** because of the mismanagement of their books.

To use the **bond** to pay, is execution of law (debt/death). To use the **note** to pay is operation in faith. The note is the tangible substance that carries intrinsic value. The note is the Promise of Abraham. The promise that you will have more even than you can receive.

Operation of law requires the discernment of mind.

Ask a homeless man how much a roof is worth to him and he will say it is priceless. Not because roofs are monetarily priceless, but because a roof has intrinsic value to him. The law is just the same. The letter of the law killeth but the spirit of the law giveth life.

The law will always fall short as a method of value

because everybody has his own opinion. The government says that one hundred dollar bills are worth a hundred dollars, but my grocer won't take bills that large. To the grocer, money over fifty dollars isn't worth a cent.

Everybody has his own opinion. Its his business, not mine. But when people get involved in your business, apply public policy to the account.

Under public policy debt can't be used to pay a debt. Whoever claims a value other than the intrinsic value of remedy is in disregard of public policy; Grace.

Creditors: Love thy debtors as thyself and allow the other party to operate in accordance with public policy.

Everybody's policy should be to act in accordance with public policy when you make an acceptance, but this is not so. The policy of the public is to disregard public policy, whenever they can get away with it.

When the promise is **"passed over"** it appears as though the offeror is billing me as though I am the surety of the bond. When they write a bill (a check to me) and don't make any deposit (and "pass over" the bank) they will overdraft my account every time. This happens when the offeror bills and overdrafts me for the value of his claim. The overdraft is a **"pass over"** just like bouncing a check.

When they **"pass over"** the promise by labeling me their bond, they are indebting themselves to me, the acceptor of the charge. When he overdraft against me, and I accept, my acceptance becomes a loan of my **credit** to him. Overdrafting is an extension of credit that is treated as a loan, not a negative deposit.

Prepayment of the product, according to public policy, occurs when the product is initially created in fact. The last words of Christ, prior to His expiring on the cross, was **"It is finished."** It was the fulfillment of the law; the fulfillment of all payments, in deed.

The Industrial Society says, **"It is finished,"** when one more car comes off the assembly line. The manufacturing of the product is the **prepayment** of and for it in fact.

The United States Corporation is a team effort. We need to live, therefore people have to produce. Nothing stops. The value structure of today adjusts from that of money to that of the substance of **remedy** for survival.

"Study to be quiet, and to do your own business, and to work with your own hands, as we commanded you; That ye may walk honestly toward them that are without, and that ye may have lack of nothing." — 1 Thess. 4:11.

32
Redemption & Jubilee

In the Old Testament, Under Mosaic Law, **Jubilee** occurs every 50 years, and a **release** of debt is made every 7 years. (See Deuteronomy 15, and Leviticus 25). The debt is **discharged** and the property is returned to its owner.

In the New Testament, under Grace, Redemption occurs at every acceptance of the charge, in a twinkling of an eye. The opening and closing of the account is simultaneous.

"In a moment, in the twinkling of an eye, at the last trump : for the trumpet shall sound, and the dead (debtors) *shall be raised incorruptible* (debt free)*, and we shall be changed."* — 1 Corinthians 15:52.

And we shall be changed from debtors to creditors by commercial redemption for there is no bondage under the law, in Grace. (All debt is discharged in bankruptcy reorganization).

When debts are redeemed, the credit returns from the user to the owner, and the debt is "wiped" clean. The debt is charged-off and the account is adjusted thereby.

You become a redeemer of monetary substance and debt, in emulation of the true Redeemer, Christ, by your acceptance of unlimited liability for the charge.

Public Policy is Grace. The Law has been fulfilled through HJR 192. HJR 192 makes it against Public

Policy to require payment for a debt. Debts are "discharged" (forgiven by the government) instead.

In Commercial Redemption the debt-account is closed at the acceptance of the charge. The interest (credit) is returned to the principle (principal) for the adjustment of the account. The return is a "tax-return".

In the Commercial Process of Redemption (CPR) you are the original owner of your credit. You are redeeming **your** credit (your property) that the industrial society, the Public, attempts to "escheat" from you.

ESCHEAT: **"Reversion of property to the state upon the death of the owner when no Will has been declared."**

In a debt driven society, you are considered to be dead (in debt) under the law, and if you haven't expressed your "Will" — your intent to claim your exemption (the blessing offered for your obedience to God's Law) — the public attempts to "escheat" your blessing (your exemption) from you instead.

Your are being "cheated" out of your inheritance as a Child of God, wherein your *"ignor-ance of the Law"* is no excuse.

THE TEN MAXIMS OF COMMERCIAL LAW

10 MAXIMS OF LAW

1. A workman is worthy of his hire.

2. All men are equal under the law.

3. In commerce truth is sovereign.

4. Truth is expressed in the form of an affidavit.

5. An unrebutted affidavit stands as truth in commerce.

6. An unrebutted affidavit becomes judgement in commerce.

7. A matter must be expressed to be resolved.

8. He who leaves the field of battle first loses by default.

9. Sacrifice is the measure of credibility

10. A lien or claim can be satisfied only through rebuttal by counter affidavit point by point, resolution by jury, or payment or performance of the claim.

10 MAXIMS OF LAW

1. *Exodus 20:15; Lev. 19:13; Mat. 10:10; Luke 10:7; II Tim. 2:6.*

2. *God's Law; Natural and Moral law; Exodus 21:23-25; Lev. 24: 17-21; Deut. 1:17, 19:21; Mat. 22:36-40; Luke 10:17; Col. 3:25.*

3. *Exodus 20:16; Ps. 117:2; John 8:32; II Cor. 13:8.*

4. *Lev. 5:4-5; Lev. 6:3-5; Lev. 19:11-13: Num. 30:2; Mat. 5:33; James 5:12.*

5. *1 Pet. 1:25; Heb. 6:13-15.*

6. *Heb. 6:16-17.*

7. *Heb. 4:16; Phil. 4:6; Eph. 6:19-21.*

8. *Book of Job; Mat. 10:22.*

9. *No willingness to sacrifice = no liability, responsibility, authority or measure of conviction; "nothing ventured nothing gained."*

10. *Gen. 2-3; Matthew 4; Revelation.*

33
More Maxims of Law

1. A payment tendered and refused is paid in full. (see page 83)

2. The Offeror is the tail and the Acceptor is the head. (see page 83)

3. You must go low to be made high. (see page 83 &104)

4. An offer refuse is dishonored. (see page 83)

5. An offer commands a response. (see page 83)

6. Creditors never lose; debtors never win. (see page104)

7. You must give honor to get honor. (see page104)

8. He who has the gold pays the debts. (see page106)

9. No one can be compelled to do the impossible. (see page106)

10 HJR 192 of 1933 is public policy. (see page106)

11. A contract is a bond. (see page107)

12. A bond is a contract. (see page107)

13. Public policy is an unbeatable contract bond. (see page107)

14. The created is subject to the creator. (see page124)

15. The borrower is subject to the lender. (see page124)

16. The slave is subject to the master. (see page124)

17. The debtor is subject to the creditor. (see page 124)

18. No controversy can exist in bankruptcy.

19. Creating a controversy is a dishonor.

20. All debts are forgiven in bankrupcy.

21. An offer of legal tender cannot be refused.

22. The refusal of legal tender is a debt discharged.

23. Refusing to accept payment on a debt cancels the debt.

24. The validity of the public debt shall not be questioned. (U.S. Constitution, Amendment 14, Section 4).

25. All debt must be either accepted and discharged or paid with notes.

Amendment XIV

Section 4. The validity of the public debt shall not be questioned.

— *United States Constitution*

www.ingramcontent.com/pod-product-compliance
Lightning Source LLC
LaVergne TN
LVHW021944130325
805898LV00001B/210